Crime Fiction
A short story collection

Crime Fiction

A short story collection

Annotationen und Auswahl
der Texte und Zusatztexte
von Isabelle Richter

Ernst Klett Sprachen
Stuttgart

Bildnachweis:
6 Thinkstock (GeorgiosArt), München; **7** Thinkstock (Photos.com),
München; **8** Universal Art Archive / Alamy Stock Foto; **12** Thinkstock
(Photos.com), München; **39** Thinkstock (Photos.com), München; **67**
Baker Street Scans / Alamy Stock Foto; **74** Baker Street Scans / Alamy
Stock Foto; **81** Baker Street Scans / Alamy Stock Foto; **90** Baker Street
Scans / Alamy Stock Foto; **91** ullstein bild - Lebrecht Music & Arts

1. Auflage 1 ⁶ ⁵ ⁴ ³ ² | 2020 19 18 17 16

This edition © Ernst Klett Sprachen GmbH, Rotebühlstraße 77,
70178 Stuttgart 2015.
Alle Rechte vorbehalten.
www.klett-sprachen.de

Worterklärungen von Isabelle Richter
Redaktion: Paul Newcomb
Layoutkonzeption: Elmar Feuerbach, Sandra Vrabec
Gestaltung und Satz: bostext, 71292 Friolzheim
Umschlaggestaltung und Illustration: Maja Smrcek
Druck und Bindung: Medienhaus Plump GmbH, Rheinbreitbach

Printed in Germany

ISBN 978-3-12-534642-0

Contents

Abbreviations used in annotations

abb	abbreviation	*mus*	music
adj	adjective	*off*	offensive (very rude!)
AE	American English	*old*	old-fashioned
BE	British English	*opp of*	opposite of
ca.	circa	*pl*	plural
coll	colloquial	*Rel*	Religion
fig	figurative	*sb*	somebody
fml	formal	*sl*	slang (*inf* language
Fr	French		that not everybody
hist	history		understands)
idm	idiom	*sth*	something
inf	informal	*usu*	usually
Lat	Latin		

I. Victorian Detective Fiction: An Introduction

by Christopher Pittard

A new kind of anxiety about the nature of crime was brought about by the changing nature of
5 society in the late eighteenth century. The industrial revolution brought about not only the growth of the city (by 1851, over half of the population of Britain
10 was located in urban areas), but also an economy which was beginning to set more value by its portable property than land. The theft of property thus became a
15 real threat, especially in an environment where thousands of people were living in close proximity. The establishment of the Metropolitan Police in 1828
20 answered some of these anxieties – it also created the figure of the official police detective.

Home Secretary Sir Robert Peel (1788–1850) established the Metropolitan Police as London's first full-time, professional, law-enforcment body. The first policemen were sometimes known as "peelers".

Although fiction dealing with crime and mystery had been published well before the Victorian age, crime literature before
25 1800 had frequently focused on the criminal as the sympathetic hero. […] By the start of the nineteenth century, then, crime writing was not only beginning to focus more on the mechanism of justice, but was becoming constructed as a commercial

13 **portable** easily movable – 14 **theft** stealing

literature of relaxation. […] The focus shifted from the criminals to those who captured the criminals, and the rise of a literature of detection.

It would not be until the middle of the nineteenth century that the police detective made his literary debut. Although contemporary analyses of 'classic' detective fiction have often been concerned with the construction of 'Englishness' in the genre, the Victorian detective story was influenced by the work of overseas practitioners.

The most notable of these, was, of course, Edgar Allan Poe, and his trio of stories featuring the Parisian detective Dupin. Each of the stories are significant for study of the development of the detection genre. The first, *The Murders in the Rue Morgue*, (1841) pioneered the sub-genre of the 'locked room' mystery by presenting a seemingly impossible crime with a surprising solution […] The second story, *The Mystery of Marie Roget* (1843) is interesting both historically and structurally; historically, because the story is based upon the real New York murder case of Mary Rogers; structurally, because the narrative's use of newspaper reports and textual sources anticipates the kind of fragmentary structure that would be used by Wilkie Collins in *The Woman in White* (1860). *The Purloined Letter* (1845) has become significant in terms of psychoanalytic theory, following Jacques Lacan's analysis of the story […]. But in a wider sense the stories are significant for introducing us to the figure of the detective in Dupin. Dupin would be a template for many of the detectives to appear in

Wilkie Collins (1824–1889)

---

9 **practitioner** [præk'tɪʃⁿəʳ] a professional (*here:* authors) – 27 **Jacques Lacan** (1901–1981) was an influential French psychoanalyst and psychiatrist. – 33 **template** model

the late nineteenth century, in particular Sherlock Holmes (who repays the favour by dismissing Dupin as a 'very
5 inferior fellow' in *A Study in Scarlet*), by placing an emphasis on intellect and ratiocination. [...]

The first British literary
10 detective, however, would not appear until 1852. Charles Dickens' novel *Bleak House*, presented Inspector Bucket, the detective who solves
15 the murder of the lawyer Tulkinghorn. With Bucket, Dickens at once created the prototype of the literary detective, and emphasised his
20 uncertain status in society, as the figure who stands halfway

The stories that comprised The Adventures of Sherlock Holmes, including A Scandal in Bohemia, first appeared together in The Strand Magazine between June 1891 and July 1892.

between respectable society and the criminals (who would, by the end of the nineteenth century, become configured as a race apart). Like Dupin, Bucket has an air of omniscience, and while
25 not quite arrogant, his confrontation of Sir Leicester Dedlock during the course of his investigation is certainly self-assured. Yet there is not the same emphasis on purely intellectual detection; Bucket is only able to solve the mystery because he knows the city of London intimately, and can cross the
30 boundaries the text presents, not only socially but in terms of the novel's structure of two narrations. [...]

Yet although the official detective had made a literary appearance, the rise of a new form of crime fiction after the

---

8 **ratiocination** *(old)* reasoning – 24 **omniscience** having unlimited knowledge and understanding

mid-century put the emphasis firmly on the amateur sleuth and, at times, back onto the criminal. […]

[Wilkie Collins's] *The Woman in White* is considered to be the first of the sensation novels, but his later work would indicate
5 a move towards detective fiction. *The Moonstone*, published in 1868 (coincidentally, the year of the final public hanging in Britain), employed many of the techniques of sensation fiction, but was more oriented towards the solving of a central puzzle, whereas the mystery of earlier sensation fiction had often been
10 concerned with an undefined 'secret'. […]

By the last fifteen years of Victoria's reign, detective fiction had become established as a genre in its own right, and one with a huge readership […]. Although the publication of detective novels did not dwindle in the final decade of the nineteenth
15 century, modern studies of the genre tend to identify this period as the 'golden age' of the short story of detection […]. The characterisation of the fin de siècle as the age of the short story of detection is in no small part the work of *The Strand* Magazine. *The Strand* was launched in 1891 by George Newnes, an editor
20 who had already experienced considerable commercial success with the periodical *Tit-Bits*. Newnes' acute business sense, combined with a kind of public paternalism […], suggested that the new magazine was guaranteed at least a degree of success, as well as providing the reading public with what Newnes
25 described in the first issue as 'cheap, healthful literature'. Such literature included regular 'Illustrated Interviews', 'Portraits of Celebrities at Different Times of their Lives' (with a significant emphasis on illustrations, as a display of publishing ability) – and detective stories. The first issue, surprisingly, was without
30 fictitious crime (although it included an article entitled *A Night with the Thames Police*), but by the second issue Grant Allen had provided the Strand's first detective story, *Jerry Stokes*. Later in 1891, Conan Doyle began the series *The Adventures of Sherlock*

1 **sleuth** [slu:θ] detective – 14 **to dwindle** to decrease

Holmes, presenting the first short stories of the detective he had introduced in Mrs Beeton's Christmas Annual for 1887. [...]

5   The work of criminal anthropologists such as Cesare Lombroso and Havelock Ellis towards the end of the nineteenth century located the tendency to criminality in the body, and even literary and artistic criticism such as Max Nordau's *Degeneration* (1892) fuelled fears that if Darwinian evolution could go forward, it could also go backwards. The criminal became a throwback to a more savage age, and crime itself became a social disease to
10 be treated by the doctor detective.

7 **to fuel** [fju:l] *(here: fig)* to increase

II. The Stories

Edgar Allan Poe (1809–1849)

1. "The Tell-Tale Heart" (1843)
2. "The Purloined Letter" (1845) (slightly abridged)

Arthur Conan Doyle (1859–1930)

3. "A Study in Scarlet" (1886) (the first two chapters)
4. "A Scandal in Bohemia" (1891)

P.D. James (1920–2014)

5. The Part-Time Job (2010)

Edgar Allan Poe (1809–1849)

Edgar Allan Poe (right) was a famous American author of the Romantic and Gothic Era,
5 artistic and literary movements of the late 18th and early 19th century. He became widely known not only for his poetry (e.g. *The Raven*, 1845) but also
10 for his tales of mystery and the macabre, being one of the first authors to explore the short story genre.

As the creator of the iconic
15 character, C. Auguste Dupin, his Parisian amateur detective, Poe is also considered one of the inventors of detective fiction, or what he called "tales of ratiocination" (= reasoning). He greatly influenced contemporary
20 authors and later fellow writers of detective fiction, such as Sir Arthur Conan Doyle.

While *The Tell-Tale Heart* (1843) is an example of classic Gothic fiction, his short story *The Purloined Letter*, published in 1845 (and reprinted in this collection on page 20), featuring Dupin's
25 third case, can be regarded as an early forerunner of the modern detective story.

Story 1: The Tell-Tale Heart (1843)

by Edgar Allan Poe

[Editor's note: Although some punctuation and orthography has been changed to make the story more accessible to the modern
5 *reader, all vocabulary remains as in the original.]*

True! – Nervous – very, very dreadfully nervous I had been and am; but why will you say that I am mad? The disease had sharpened my senses – not destroyed – not dulled them. Above all was the sense of hearing acute. I heard all things in the heaven
10 and in the earth. I heard many things in hell. How, then, am I mad? Hearken! and observe how healthily – how calmly I can tell you the whole story.

It is impossible to say how first the idea entered my brain; but once conceived, it haunted me day and night. Object there was
15 none. Passion there was none. I loved the old man. He had never wronged me. He had never given me insult. For his gold I had no desire. I think it was his eye! Yes, it was this! He had the eye of a vulture – a pale blue eye, with a film over it. Whenever it fell upon me, my blood ran cold; and so by degrees – very gradually
20 – I made up my mind to take the life of the old man, and thus rid myself of the eye forever.

Now this is the point. You fancy me mad. Madmen know nothing. But you should have seen me. You should have seen how wisely I proceeded – with what caution – with what foresight
25 – with what dissimulation I went to work! I was never kinder to the old man than during the whole week before I killed him. And every night, about midnight, I turned the latch of his door and opened it – oh so gently! And then, when I had made an

---

8 **to dull** to wear out, to suppress – 9 **acute** precise, very good – 11 **Hearken!** *(old)* Listen! – 18 **vulture** *Geier* – 21 **to rid sb of sth** to relieve sb of sth *(etwas für jdn beseitigen)* – 22 **You fancy me mad.** You think I am mad. – 25 **dissimulation** secrecy – 27 **latch** *Klinke*

opening sufficient for my head, I put in a dark lantern, all closed, closed, that no light shone out, and then I thrust in my head. Oh, you would have laughed to see how cunningly I thrust it in! I moved it slowly – very, very slowly, so that I might not disturb
5 the old man's sleep. It took me an hour to place my whole head within the opening so far that I could see him as he lay upon his bed. Ha! Would a madman have been so wise as this, And then, when my head was well in the room, I undid the lantern cautiously – oh, so cautiously – cautiously (for the hinges creaked)
10 – I undid it just so much that a single thin ray fell upon the vulture eye. And this I did for seven long nights – every night just at midnight – but I found the eye always closed; and so it was impossible to do the work; for it was not the old man who vexed me, but his Evil Eye. And every morning, when the day
15 broke, I went boldly into the chamber, and spoke courageously to him, calling him by name in a hearty tone, and inquiring how he has passed the night. So you see he would have been a very profound old man, indeed, to suspect that every night, just at twelve, I looked in upon him while he slept.

20 Upon the eighth night I was more than usually cautious in opening the door. A watch's minute hand moves more quickly than did mine. Never before that night had I felt the extent of my own powers – of my sagacity. I could scarcely contain my feelings of triumph. To think that there I was, opening the door,
25 little by little, and he not even to dream of my secret deeds or thoughts. I fairly chuckled at the idea; and perhaps he heard me; for he moved on the bed suddenly, as if startled. Now you may think that I drew back – but no. His room was as black as pitch with the thick darkness, (for the shutters were close
30 fastened, through fear of robbers), and so I knew that he could not see the opening of the door, and I kept pushing it on steadily, steadily.

3 **cunningly** cleverly – 9 **hinges** ['hɪndʒɪz] (of a door) *Türangeln (hier: der Laternenöffnung)* – 14 **to vex sb** *(old)* to annoy sb – 16 **to inquire** to ask – 18 **profound** *(old)* clever, observant – 23 **sagacity** [sə'gæsəti] *(old)* intelligence – 23 **scarcely** hardly – 26 **to chuckle** to giggle, to laugh – 27 **startled** surprised, shocked – 28 **black as pitch** *pechschwarz*

I had my head in, and was about to open the lantern, when my thumb slipped upon the tin fastening, and the old man sprang up in bed, crying out – "Who's there?"

I kept quite still and said nothing. For a whole hour I did not
5   move a muscle, and in the meantime I did not hear him lie down. He was still sitting up in the bed listening; just as I have done, night after night, hearkening to the death watches in the wall.

Presently I heard a slight groan, and I knew it was the groan
10   of mortal terror. It was not a groan of pain or of grief – oh, no! – It was the low stifled sound that arises from the bottom of the soul when overcharged with awe. I knew the sound well. Many a night, just at midnight, when all the world slept, it has welled up from my own bosom, deepening, with its dreadful echo, the
15   terrors that distracted me. I say I knew it well. I knew what the old man felt, and pitied him, although I chuckled at heart. I knew that he had been lying awake ever since the first slight noise, when he had turned in the bed. His fears had been ever since growing upon him. He had been trying to fancy them
20   causeless, but could not. He had been saying to himself – "It is nothing but the wind in the chimney – it is only a mouse crossing the floor," or "It is merely a cricket which has made a single chirp." Yes, he had been trying to comfort himself with these suppositions: but he had found all in vain. All in vain; because
25   Death, in approaching him had stalked with his black shadow before him, and enveloped the victim. And it was the mournful influence of the unperceived shadow that caused him to feel – although he neither saw nor heard – to feel the presence of my head within the room.

30   When I had waited a long time, very patiently, without hearing him lie down, I resolved to open a little – a very, very little – crevice in the lantern. So I opened it – you cannot imagine how

---

11 **stifled** suppressed – 22 **cricket** *Grille* – 24 **in vain** for nothing – 26 **mournful** sad –
27 **unperceived** unseen – 32 **crevice** *here:* opening

stealthily, stealthily – until, at length a simple dim ray, like the thread of the spider, shot from out the crevice and fell full upon the vulture eye.

It was open – wide, wide open – and I grew furious as I gazed
5 upon it. I saw it with perfect distinctness – all a dull blue, with a hideous veil over it that chilled the very marrow in my bones; but I could see nothing else of the old man's face or person: for I had directed the ray as if by instinct, precisely upon the damned spot.

10 And have I not told you that what you mistake for madness is but over-acuteness of the sense? Now, I say, there came to my ears a low, dull, quick sound, such as a watch makes when enveloped in cotton. I knew that sound well, too. It was the beating of the old man's heart. It increased my fury, as the beating
15 of a drum stimulates the soldier into courage.

But even yet I refrained and kept still. I scarcely breathed. I held the lantern motionless. I tried how steadily I could maintain the ray upon the eye. Meantime the hellish tattoo of the heart increased. It grew quicker and quicker, and louder and louder
20 every instant. The old man's terror must have been extreme! It grew louder, I say, louder every moment! Do you mark me well I have told you that I am nervous: so I am. And now at the dead hour of the night, amid the dreadful silence of that old house, so strange a noise as this excited me to uncontrollable terror.
25 Yet, for some minutes longer I refrained and stood still. But the beating grew louder, louder! I thought the heart must burst. And now a new anxiety seized me – the sound would be heard by a neighbour! The old man's hour had come! With a loud yell, I threw open the lantern and leaped into the room. He shrieked
30 once – once only. In an instant I dragged him to the floor, and pulled the heavy bed over him. I then smiled gaily, to find the

---

1 **stealthily** [ˈstelθɪli] secretly, quietly – 5 **distinctness** clarity – 6 **hideous** [ˈhɪdiəs] disgusting – 6 **veil** [veɪl] *Schleier* – 6 **(bone) marrow** *Knochenmark* – 16 **to refrain** *(here: old)* to not do sth – 18 **tattoo** *(old)* regular sound of drumbeats – 27 **anxiety** [æŋˈzaɪəti] panic, worry – 29 **to leap** to rush, to jump – 31 **gaily** happily

deed so far done. But, for many minutes, the heart beat on with a muffled sound. This, however, did not vex me; it would not be heard through the wall. At length it ceased. The old man was dead. I removed the bed and examined the corpse. Yes, he was

5 stone, stone dead. I placed my hand upon the heart and held it there many minutes. There was no pulsation. He was stone dead. His eye would trouble me no more.

If still you think me mad, you will think so no longer when I describe the wise precautions I took for the concealment of the

10 body. The night waned, and I worked hastily, but in silence. First of all I dismembered the corpse. I cut off the head and the arms and the legs.

I then took up three planks from the flooring of the chamber, and deposited all between the scantlings. I then replaced the

15 boards so cleverly, so cunningly, that no human eye – not even his – could have detected any thing wrong. There was nothing to wash out – no stain of any kind – no blood-spot whatever. I had been too wary for that. A tub had caught all – ha! ha!

When I had made an end of these labors, it was four o'clock

20 – still dark as midnight. As the bell sounded the hour, there came a knocking at the street door. I went down to open it with a light heart – for what had I now to fear? There entered three men, who introduced themselves, with perfect suavity, as officers of the police. A shriek had been heard by a neighbour during the

25 night; suspicion of foul play had been aroused; information had been lodged at the police office, and they (the officers) had been deputed to search the premises.

I smiled – for what had I to fear? I bade the gentlemen welcome. The shriek, I said, was my own in a dream. The old man, I

30 mentioned, was absent in the country. I took my visitors all over

---

3 **to cease** to stop – 9 **concealment** hiding – 10 **to wane** (old) to come to an end – 11 **to dismember** (old) to take apart – 14 **scantlings** (old) floorboards – 18 **wary** careful – 19 **labors** work, jobs – 23 **suavity** ['swɑːvəti] politeness – 27 **deputed** (old) sent – 27 **premises** the house and its grounds – 28 **to bid [bade, bidden] sb welcome** (old) to welcome sb, to invite sb to do sth

the house. I bade them search – search well. I led them, at length, to his chamber. I showed them his treasures, secure, undisturbed. In the enthusiasm of my confidence, I brought chairs into the room, and desired them here to rest from their fatigues, while 5 I myself, in the wild audacity of my perfect triumph, placed my own seat upon the very spot beneath which reposed the corpse of the victim.

The officers were satisfied. My manner had convinced them. I was singularly at ease. They sat, and while I answered cheerily, 10 they chatted of familiar things. But, ere long, I felt myself getting pale and wished them gone. My head ached, and I fancied a ringing in my ears: but still they sat and still chatted. The ringing became more distinct; it continued and became more distinct: I talked more freely to get rid of the feeling, but it continued 15 and gained definiteness – until, at length, I found that the noise was not within my ears.

No doubt I now grew very pale, but I talked more fluently, and with a heightened voice. Yet the sound increased – and what could I do? It was a low, dull, quick sound – much such a sound 20 as a watch makes when enveloped in cotton. I gasped for breath – and yet the officers heard it not. I talked more quickly – more vehemently; but the noise steadily increased. I arose and argued about trifles, in a high key and with violent gesticulations; but the noise steadily increased. Why would they not be gone? I 25 paced the floor to and fro with heavy strides, as if excited to fury by the observations of the men – but the noise steadily increased. Oh God! What could I do? I foamed – I raved – I swore! I swung the chair upon which I had been sitting, and grated it upon the boards, but the noise arose over all and continually increased. 30 It grew louder – louder – louder! And still the men chatted

---

4 **fatigues** *here:* efforts, hard work – 5 **audacity** *Kühnheit* – 9 **at ease** light-hearted, untroubled – 10 **ere** [eə] **long** before long, soon – 18 **heightened** louder – 23 **trifles** unimportant things – 23 **high key** high-pitched voice – 25 **to pace to and fro** to walk up and down – 27 **to foam** *schäumen* – 27 **to rave** to talk wildly – 28 **to grate** *hier: mit einem kratzenden Geräusch über den Boden bewegen*

pleasantly, and smiled. Was it possible they heard not? Almighty God! – No, no! They heard! They suspected! They knew! They were making a mockery of my horror! This I thought, and this I think. But anything was better than this agony! Anything was
5 more tolerable than this derision! I could bear those hypocritical smiles no longer! I felt that I must scream or die! And now – again! Hark! Louder! Louder! Louder! Louder!

"Villains!" I shrieked, "dissemble no more! I admit the deed! – Tear up the planks! Here, here! – It is the beating of his hideous
10 heart!"

Personification

– THE END –

---

3 **to make a mockery of sth** to ridicule sth – 4 **agony** extreme pain – 5 **derision** *Hohn, Spott* – 5 **hypocritical** [ˌhɪpəˈkrɪtɪkəl] *heuchlerisch* – 8 **villain** evil person – 8 **to dissemble** to hide, to put on an act

Story 2: The Purloined Letter (1845)

by Edgar Allan Poe

[Editor's note: Although some punctuation and orthography has been changed to make the story more accessible to the modern
5 *reader, all vocabulary remains as in the original.]*

Nil sapientiae odiosius acumine nimio. – Seneca.

At Paris, just after dark one gusty evening in the autumn of 18--, I was enjoying the twofold luxury of meditation and a meerschaum, in company with my friend C. Auguste Dupin, in
10 his little back library, or book-closet, au troisieme, No. 33, Rue Dunot, Faubourg St. Germain. For one hour at least we had maintained a profound silence; while each, to any casual observer, might have seemed intently and exclusively occupied with the curling eddies of smoke that oppressed the atmosphere
15 of the chamber. For myself, however, I was mentally discussing certain topics which had formed matter for conversation between us at an earlier period of the evening; I mean the affair of the Rue Morgue, and the mystery attending the murder of Marie Roget. I looked upon it, therefore, as something of a coincidence,
20 when the door of our apartment was thrown open and admitted our old acquaintance, Monsieur G – , the Prefect of the Parisian police.

We gave him a hearty welcome; for there was nearly half as much of the entertaining as of the contemptible about the man,

---

6 **Nil sapientiae odiosius acumine nimio.** *(Lat)* "Nothing is more hateful to wisdom than excessive cleverness." – 6 **Seneca** (ca. 4 BC–AD 65) Roman philosopher and statesman – 7 **gusty** windy, stormy – 9 **meerschaum** pipe (for smoking) – 10 **au troisieme** *(Fr)* on the third floor – 11 **Faubourg St. Germain** historic, wealthy district of Paris – 14 **eddy** whirl – 18 **affair of the Rue Morgue** reference to Dupin's first case in "The Murders at the Rue Morgue" (1841) – 18 **Marie Roget** reference to Dupin's second case in "The Mystery of Marie Rogêt" (1842) – 24 **contemptible** despicable *(verachtenswert)*

and we had not seen him for several years. We had been sitting in the dark, and Dupin now arose for the purpose of lighting a lamp, but sat down again, without doing so, upon G.'s saying that he had called to consult us, or rather to ask the opinion of my friend, about some official business which had occasioned a great deal of trouble.

"If it is any point requiring reflection," observed Dupin, as he forbore to enkindle the wick, "we shall examine it to better purpose in the dark."

"That is another of your odd notions," said the Prefect, who had a fashion of calling every thing "odd" that was beyond his comprehension, and thus lived amid an absolute legion of "oddities."

"Very true," said Dupin, as he supplied his visitor with a pipe, and rolled towards him a comfortable chair.

"And what is the difficulty now?" I asked. "Nothing more in the assassination way, I hope?"

"Oh no, nothing of that nature. The fact is, the business is very simple indeed, and I make no doubt that we can manage it sufficiently well ourselves; but then I thought Dupin would like to hear the details of it, because it is so excessively odd."

"Simple and odd," said Dupin.

"Why, yes; and not exactly that, either. The fact is, we have all been a good deal puzzled because the affair is so simple, and yet baffles us altogether."

"Perhaps it is the very simplicity of the thing which puts you at fault," said my friend.

"What nonsense you do talk!" replied the Prefect, laughing heartily.

"Perhaps the mystery is a little too plain," said Dupin.

"Oh, good heavens! who ever heard of such an idea?"

"A little too self-evident."

5 **to occasion** to cause – 8 **to forbear [forbore, forborne]** *(old)* to refrain from doing sth, to do without – 8 **to enkindle** to set fire to – 8 **wick** *Docht* – 25 **to baffle** to confuse, to amaze

"Ha! Ha! Ha! – Ha! Ha! Ha! – Ho! Ho! Ho!" roared our visitor, profoundly amused, "oh, Dupin, you will be the death of me yet!"

"And what, after all, is the matter on hand?" I asked.

5 "Why, I will tell you," replied the Prefect, as he gave a long, steady, and contemplative puff, and settled himself in his chair. "I will tell you in a few words; but, before I begin, let me caution you that this is an affair demanding the greatest secrecy, and that I should most probably lose the position I now hold, were

10 it known that I confided it to any one.

"Proceed," said I.

"Or not," said Dupin.

"Well, then; I have received personal information, from a very high quarter, that a certain document of the last importance,

15 has been purloined from the royal apartments. The individual who purloined it is known; this beyond a doubt; he was seen to take it. It is known, also, that it still remains in his possession."

"How is this known?" asked Dupin.

20 "It is clearly inferred," replied the Prefect, "from the nature of the document, and from the nonappearance of certain results which would at once arise from its passing out of the robber's possession; that is to say, from his employing it as he must design in the end to employ it."

25 "Be a little more explicit," I said.

"Well, I may venture so far as to say that the paper gives its holder a certain power in a certain quarter where such power is immensely valuable." The Prefect was fond of the cant of diplomacy.

30 "Still I do not quite understand," said Dupin.

"No? Well, the disclosure of the document to a third person, who shall be nameless, would bring in question the honor of a

---

1 **to roar** to speak very loudly – 13 **from a very high quarter** from sb in a high and important social position – 15 **to purloin** to steal – 20 **to infer** to conclude – 23 **to employ** to use – 26 **to venture** to dare – 28 **cant** technical and pompous jargon

personage of most exalted station; and this fact gives the holder of the document an ascendancy over the illustrious personage whose honor and peace are so jeopardized."

"But this ascendancy," I interposed, "would depend upon the
5 robber's knowledge of the loser's knowledge of the robber. Who would dare – "

"The thief," said G., "is the Minister D– , who dares all things, those unbecoming as well as those becoming a man. The method of the theft was not less ingenious than bold. The document in
10 question – a letter, to be frank – had been received by the personage robbed while alone in the royal boudoir. During its perusal she was suddenly interrupted by the entrance of the other exalted personage from whom especially it was her wish to conceal it. After a hurried and vain endeavor to thrust it in a
15 drawer, she was forced to place it, open as it was, upon a table. The address, however, was uppermost, and, the contents thus unexposed, the letter escaped notice. At this juncture enters the Minister D– . His lynx eye immediately perceives the paper, recognises the handwriting of the address, observes the
20 confusion of the personage addressed, and fathoms her secret. After some business transactions, hurried through in his ordinary manner, he produces a letter somewhat similar to the one in question, opens it, pretends to read it, and then places it in close juxtaposition to the other. Again he converses, for some fifteen
25 minutes, upon the public affairs. At length, in taking leave, he takes also from the table the letter to which he had no claim. Its rightful owner saw, but, of course, dared not call attention to the act, in the presence of the third personage who stood at her elbow. The minister decamped; leaving his own letter – one
30 of no importance – upon the table."

1 **of most exalted station** in a high social position – 2 **ascendancy** [ə'sendəntsi] domination, power – 3 **to jeopardize** ['dʒepədaɪz] to endanger – 8 **unbecoming** unseemly, not flattering – 11 **boudoir** *(Fr)* a woman's private sitting room – 12 **perusal** [pə'ruːzᵊl] examination – 17 **juncture** particularly important moment – 18 **lynx** [lɪnks] *Luchs* – 24 **in close juxtaposition** *here:* very close to – 29 **to decamp** to leave secretly

"Here, then," said Dupin to me, "you have precisely what you demand to make the ascendancy complete – the robber's knowledge of the loser's knowledge of the robber."

"Yes," replied the Prefect, "and the power thus attained has,
5 for some months past, been wielded, for political purposes, to a very dangerous extent. The personage robbed is more thoroughly convinced, every day, of the necessity of reclaiming her letter. But this, of course, cannot be done openly. In fine, driven to despair, she has committed the matter to me."

10 "Than whom," said Dupin, amid a perfect whirlwind of smoke, "no more sagacious agent could, I suppose, be desired, or even imagined."

"You flatter me," replied the Prefect, "but it is possible that some such opinion may have been entertained."

15 "It is clear," said I, "as you observe, that the letter is still in possession of the minister; since it is this possession, and not any employment of the letter, which bestows the power. With the employment the power departs."

"True," said G. "and upon this conviction I proceeded. My first
20 care was to make thorough search of the minister's hotel; and here my chief embarrassment lay in the necessity of searching without his knowledge. Beyond all things, I have been warned of the danger which would result from giving him reason to suspect our design."

25 "But," said I, "you are quite au fait in these investigations. The Parisian police have done this thing often before."

"Oh yes, and for this reason I did not despair. The habits of the minister gave me, too, a great advantage. He is frequently absent from home all night. His servants are by no means
30 numerous. They sleep at a distance from their master's apartment, and, being chiefly Neapolitans, are readily made drunk. I have keys, as you know, with which I can open any chamber or cabinet in Paris. For three months a night has not

---

5 **to wield power** to exercise power – 11 **sagacious** intelligent – 21 **chief** main –
24 **design** intention – 25 **to be au fait** *(Fr)* to be well-informed

passed, during the greater part of which I have not been engaged, personally, in ransacking the D– Hotel. My honor is interested, and, to mention a great secret, the reward is enormous. So I did not abandon the search until I had become fully satisfied that
5 the thief is a more astute man than myself. I fancy that I have investigated every nook and corner of the premises in which it is possible that the paper can be concealed."

"But is it not possible," I suggested, "that although the letter may be in possession of the minister, as it unquestionably is,
10 he may have concealed it elsewhere than upon his own premises?"

"This is barely possible," said Dupin. "The present peculiar condition of affairs at court, and especially of those intrigues in which D– is known to be involved, would render the instant
15 availability of the document – its susceptibility of being produced at a moment's notice – a point of nearly equal importance with its possession."

"Its susceptibility of being produced?" said I.

"That is to say, of being destroyed," said Dupin.
20 "True," I observed, "the paper is clearly then upon the premises. As for its being upon the person of the minister, we may consider that as out of the question."

"Entirely," said the Prefect. "He has been twice waylaid, as if by footpads, and his person rigorously searched under my own
25 inspection.

"You might have spared yourself this trouble," said Dupin. "D– , I presume, is not altogether a fool, and, if not, must have anticipated these waylayings, as a matter of course."

"Not altogether a fool," said G., "but then he's a poet, which
30 I take to be only one remove from a fool."

---

1 **to be engaged in sth** to concern oneself with sth – 2 **to ransack** to rob, to plunder – 5 **astute** clever – 6 **nook** *Nische* – 6 **premises** *(pl) here:* apartment – 12 **peculiar** special, particular – 15 **susceptibility** [sə‚septə'bɪləti] *here:* possibility – 23 **to waylay sb** to attack and rob sb

"True," said Dupin, after a long and thoughtful whiff from his meerschaum, "although I have been guilty of certain doggerel myself."

"Suppose you detail," said I, "the particulars of your search."

"Why the fact is, we took our time, and we searched everywhere. I have had long experience in these affairs. I took the entire building, room by room; devoting the nights of a whole week to each. We examined, first, the furniture of each apartment. We opened every possible drawer; and I presume you know that, to a properly trained police agent, such a thing as a secret drawer is impossible. Any man is a dolt who permits a 'secret' drawer to escape him in a search of this kind. The thing is so plain. There is a certain amount of bulk – of space – to be accounted for in every cabinet. Then we have accurate rules. The fiftieth part of a line could not escape us. After the cabinets we took the chairs. The cushions we probed with the fine long needles you have seen me employ. From the tables we removed the tops."

"Why so?"

"Sometimes the top of a table, or other similarly arranged piece of furniture, is removed by the person wishing to conceal an article; then the leg is excavated, the article deposited within the cavity, and the top replaced. The bottoms and tops of bedposts are employed in the same way."

"But could not the cavity be detected by sounding?" I asked.

"By no means, if, when the article is deposited, a sufficient wadding of cotton be placed around it. Besides, in our case, we were obliged to proceed without noise."

"But you could not have removed – you could not have taken to pieces all articles of furniture in which it would have been

2 **doggerel** poetry that is irregular in rhythm and rhyme to create a comic effect (*Knittelvers*) – 12 **dolt** (*inf, old*) idiot – 22 **to conceal** to hide – 23 **excavated** carved out, hollow (*hohl*) – 24 **cavity** hollow space

possible to make a deposit in the manner you mention. A letter may be compressed into a thin spiral roll, not differing much in shape or bulk from a large knitting-needle, and in this form it might be inserted into the rung of a chair, for example. You did not take to pieces all the chairs?"

"Certainly not; but we did better – we examined the rungs of every chair in the hotel, and, indeed, the jointings of every description of furniture, by the aid of a most powerful micro-scope. Had there been any traces of recent disturbance we should not have failed to detect it instantly. A single grain of gimlet-dust, for example, would have been as obvious as an apple. Any disorder in the glueing – any unusual gaping in the joints – would have sufficed to insure detection."

"I presume you looked to the mirrors, between the boards and the plates, and you probed the beds and the bed-clothes, as well as the curtains and carpets."

"That of course; and when we had absolutely completed every particle of the furniture in this way, then we examined the house itself. We divided its entire surface into compartments, which we numbered, so that none might be missed; then we scrutinized each individual square inch throughout the premises, including the two houses immediately adjoining, with the microscope, as before."

"The two houses adjoining!" I exclaimed. "You must have had a great deal of trouble."

"We had; but the reward offered is prodigious.

"You include the grounds about the houses?"

"All the grounds are paved with brick. They gave us comparatively little trouble. We examined the moss between the bricks, and found it undisturbed."

"You looked among D– ,s papers, of course, and into the books of the library?"

---

4 **rung** piece of wood between the legs of a chair which holds it together (*Sprosse*) –
7 **jointing** *(old)* wooden pieces – 10 **gimlet** small drill – 20 **to scrutinize** [ˈskruːtɪnaɪz] to
examine sth very carefully – 26 **prodigious** [prəˈdɪdʒəs] enormous

"Certainly; we opened every package and parcel; we not only opened every book, but we turned over every leaf in each volume, not contenting ourselves with a mere shake, according to the fashion of some of our police officers. We also measured the thickness of every book-cover, with the most accurate admeasurement, and applied to each the most zealous scrutiny of the microscope. Had any of the bindings been recently meddled with, it would have been utterly impossible that the fact should have escaped observation. Some five or six volumes, just from the hands of the binder, we carefully probed, longitudinally, with the needles."

"You explored the floors beneath the carpets?"

"Beyond doubt. We removed every carpet, and examined the boards with the microscope."

"And the paper on the walls?"

"Yes."

"You looked into the cellars?"

"We did."

"Then," I said, "you have been making a miscalculation, and the letter is not upon the premises, as you suppose.

"I fear you are right there," said the Prefect. "And now, Dupin, what would you advise me to do?"

"To make a thorough re-search of the premises."

"That is absolutely needless," replied G–. "I am not more sure that I breathe than I am that the letter is not at the Hotel."

"I have no better advice to give you," said Dupin. "You have, of course, an accurate description of the letter?"

"Oh yes!" And here the Prefect, producing a memorandum-book, proceeded to read aloud a minute account of the internal, and especially of the external appearance of the missing document. Soon after finishing the perusal of this description, he took his departure, more entirely depressed in spirits than I had ever known the good gentleman before.

---

11 **longitudinally** [ˌlɒndʒɪˈtjuːdɪnᵊli] lengthwise – 29 **minute** [maɪˈnjuːt] extremely precise

In about a month afterwards he paid us another visit, and found us occupied very nearly as before. He took a pipe and a chair and entered into some ordinary conversation. At length I said: "Well, but G–, what of the purloined letter? I presume you
5 have at last made up your mind that there is no such thing as overreaching the Minister?"

"Confound him, say I – yes; I made the reexamination, however, as Dupin suggested – but it was all labor lost, as I knew it would be."

10 "How much was the reward offered, did you say?" asked Dupin.

"Why, a very great deal – a very liberal reward – I don't like to say how much, precisely; but one thing I will say, that I wouldn't mind giving my individual check for fifty thousand francs to any
15 one who could obtain me that letter. The fact is, it is becoming of more and more importance every day; and the reward has been lately doubled. If it were trebled, however, I could do no more than I have done."

"Why, yes," said Dupin, drawlingly, between the whiffs of his
20 meerschaum, "I really think, G–, you have not exerted yourself … to the utmost in this matter. You might … do a little more, I think, eh?"

"How? In what way?"

"Why … puff, puff … you might … puff, puff … employ counsel
25 in the matter, eh? … Puff, puff, puff. Do you remember the story they tell of Abernethy?"

"No; hang Abernethy!"

"To be sure! Hang him and welcome. But, once upon a time, a certain rich miser conceived the design of spunging upon this
30 Abernethy for a medical opinion. Getting up, for this purpose, an ordinary conversation in a private company, he insinuated his case to the physician, as that of an imaginary individual.

---

8 **all labour lost** *(idm)* verlorene Liebesmühe – 17 **to treble** to triple – 20 **to exert oneself** to make a great effort – 29 **miser** ungenerous person – 29 **to spunge / sponge on sb** *(old)* to take advantage of sb – 31 **to insinuate** *here:* to tell

"'We will suppose," said the miser, "that his symptoms are such and such; now, doctor, what would you have directed him to take?"

"Take!" said Abernethy, "why, take advice, to be sure."

5 "But," said the Prefect, a little discomposed, "I am perfectly willing to take advice, and to pay for it. I would really give fifty thousand francs to any one who would aid me in the matter."

"In that case," replied Dupin, opening a drawer, and producing a check-book, "you may as well fill me up a check for the amount
10 mentioned. When you have signed it, I will hand you the letter."

I was astounded. The Prefect appeared absolutely thunder-stricken. For some minutes he remained speechless and motionless, looking incredulously at my friend with open
15 mouth, and eyes that seemed starting from their sockets; then, apparently in some measure, he seized a pen, and after several pauses and vacant stares, finally filled up and signed a check for fifty thousand francs, and handed it across the table to Dupin. The latter examined it carefully and deposited it in his pocket-
20 book; then, unlocking an escritoire, took thence a letter and gave it to the Prefect. This functionary grasped it in a perfect agony of joy, opened it with a trembling hand, cast a rapid glance at its contents, and then, scrambling and struggling to the door, rushed at length unceremoniously from the room and from the
25 house, without having uttered a syllable since Dupin had requested him to fill up the check.

When he had gone, my friend entered into some explanations.

"The Parisian police," he said, "are exceedingly able in their
30 way. They are persevering, ingenious, cunning, and thoroughly versed in the knowledge which their duties seem chiefly to demand. Thus, when G– detailed to us his mode of searching

---

20 **escritoire** [ˌeskriˈtwɑː] *(Fr)* writing desk – 25 **to utter** to speak – 30 **persevering** persistent, assiduous

the premises at the Hotel D– , I felt entire confidence in his having made a satisfactory investigation – so far as his labors extended."

"So far as his labors extended?" said I.

5 "Yes," said Dupin. "The measures adopted were not only the best of their kind, but carried out to absolute perfection. Had the letter been deposited within the range of their search, these fellows would, beyond a question, have found it."

I merely laughed – but he seemed quite serious in all that he
10 said.

"The measures, then," he continued, "were good in their kind, and well executed; their defect lay in their being inapplicable to the case, and to the man. A certain set of highly ingenious resources are, with the Prefect, a sort of Procrustean bed, to
15 which he forcibly adapts his designs. But he perpetually errs by being too deep or too shallow for the matter in hand; and many a schoolboy is a better reasoner than he.

[…]

All fools are poets, this the Prefect feels, and he is merely guilty
20 of a non distributio medii in thence inferring that all poets are fools."

"But is this really the poet?" I asked. "There are two brothers, I know, and both have attained reputation in letters. The Minister I believe has written learnedly on the Differential Calculus. He
25 is a mathematician, and no poet."

"You are mistaken; I know him well; he is both. As poet and mathematician, he would reason well; as mere mathematician, he could not have reasoned at all, and thus would have been at the mercy of the Prefect."

30 "You surprise me," I said, "by these opinions, which have been contradicted by the voice of the world. You do not mean to set

---

14 **Procrustean bed** arbitrary standard to which exact conformity is forced – 15 **to err** [ɜːʳ] to make a mistake – 20 **non distributio medii** *(Lat) here:* false belief –
24 **learnedly** in a scholarly, academic way – 31 **to set at naught** [nɔːt] to ignore

at naught the well-digested idea of centuries. The mathematical reason has long been regarded as the reason par excellence.

[…]

"I mean to say," continued Dupin, while I merely laughed at
5 his last observations, "that if the Minister had been no more than a mathematician, the Prefect would have been under no necessity of giving me this check. I knew him, however, as both mathematician and poet, and my measures were adapted to his capacity, with reference to the circumstances by which he was
10 surrounded. I knew him as a courtier, too, and as a bold intriguant. Such a man, I considered, could not fail to be aware of the ordinary policial modes of action. He could not have failed to anticipate – and events have proved that he did not fail to anticipate – the waylayings to which he was subjected. He must
15 have foreseen, I reflected, the secret investigations of his premises. His frequent absences from home at night, which were hailed by the Prefect as certain aids to his success, I regarded only as ruses, to afford opportunity for thorough search to the police, and thus the sooner to impress them with the conviction
20 to which G– , in fact, did finally arrive – the conviction that the letter was not upon the premises. I felt, also, that the whole train of thought, which I was at some pains in detailing to you just now, concerning the invariable principle of policial action in searches for articles concealed – I felt that this whole train of
25 thought would necessarily pass through the mind of the Minister. It would imperatively lead him to despise all the ordinary nooks of concealment. He could not, I reflected, be so weak as not to see that the most intricate and remote recess of his hotel would be as open as his commonest closets to the eyes, to the probes,
30 to the gimlets, and to the microscopes of the Prefect. I saw, in fine, that he would be driven, as a matter of course, to simplicity,

---

1 **well-digested** well thought-out – 2 **par excellence** *(Fr)* [ˌpɑːrˌeksəˈlɑːns] ultimate, best – 10 **courtier** person who practises flattery – 11 **intriguant** *(Fr)* schemer – 13 **to anticipate** to foresee – 17 **to be hailed** *here:* to be mentioned – 18 **ruse** trick – 26 **imperatively** necessarily – 28 **intricate** [ˈɪntrɪkət] *here:* difficult to find

if not deliberately induced to it as a matter of choice. You will remember, perhaps, how desperately the Prefect laughed when I suggested, upon our first interview, that it was just possible this mystery troubled him so much on account of its being so very self-evident."

"Yes," said I, "I remember his merriment well. I really thought he would have fallen into convulsions."

"The material world," continued Dupin, "abounds with very strict analogies to the immaterial; and thus some color of truth has been given to the rhetorical dogma, that metaphor, or simile, may be made to strengthen an argument, as well as to embellish a description. The principle of the vis inertiae, for example, seems to be identical in physics and metaphysics. It is not more true in the former, that a large body is with more difficulty set in motion than a smaller one, and that its subsequent momentum is commensurate with this difficulty, than it is, in the latter, that intellects of the vaster capacity, while more forcible, more constant, and more eventful in their movements than those of inferior grade, are yet the less readily moved, and more embarrassed and full of hesitation in the first few steps of their progress. Again: have you ever noticed which of the street signs, over the shop doors, are the most attractive of attention?"

"I have never given the matter a thought," I said.

"There is a game of puzzles," he resumed, "which is played upon a map. One party playing requires another to find a given word – the name of town, river, state or empire – any word, in short, upon the motley and perplexed surface of the chart. A novice in the game generally seeks to embarrass his opponents by giving them the most minutely lettered names; but the adept selects such words as stretch, in large characters, from one end of the chart to the other. These, like the over-largely lettered

---

6 **merriment** amusement – 7 **convulsions** fits of laughter – 8 **to abound with** to be full of – 11 **to embellish** *here:* to add details, decorate – 12 **vis inertiae** *(Lat)* physical principle of the force of immobility – 15 **momentum** force, swinging movement *(Schwung)* – 16 **to be commensurate with sth** to correspond with sth, to match proportionately – 27 **motley** colourful

signs and placards of the street, escape observation by dint of being excessively obvious; and here the physical oversight is precisely analogous with the moral inapprehension by which the intellect suffers to pass unnoticed those considerations which
5 are too obtrusively and too palpably self-evident. But this is a point, it appears, somewhat above or beneath the understanding of the Prefect. He never once thought it probable, or possible, that the Minister had deposited the letter immediately beneath the nose of the whole world, by way of best preventing any
10 portion of that world from perceiving it.

"But the more I reflected upon the daring, dashing, and discriminating ingenuity of D–, upon the fact that the document must always have been at hand, if he intended to use it to good purpose; and upon the decisive evidence obtained by the Prefect,
15 that it was not hidden within the limits of that dignitary's ordinary search – the more satisfied I became that, to conceal this letter, the Minister had resorted to the comprehensive and sagacious expedient of not attempting to conceal it at all.

"Full of these ideas, I prepared myself with a pair of green
20 spectacles, and called one fine morning, quite by accident, at the Ministerial hotel. I found D– at home, yawning, lounging, and dawdling, as usual, and pretending to be in the last extremity of ennui. He is, perhaps, the most really energetic human being now alive – but that is only when nobody sees him.

25 "To be even with him, I complained of my weak eyes, and lamented the necessity of the spectacles, under cover of which I cautiously and thoroughly surveyed the apartment, while seemingly intent only upon the conversation of my host.

"I paid special attention to a large writing-table near which
30 he sat, and upon which lay confusedly, some miscellaneous

---

1 **by dint of sth** through/ because of sth – 5 **obtrusively** clearly visible – 5 **palpably** clearly – 11 **dashing** *(old)* bold – 12 **discriminating** distinctive – 15 **dignitary** person of high rank – 17 **to resort to sth** to fall back upon sth, to use sth – 18 **expedient** measure – 20 **spectacles** (eye)glasses – 22 **to dawdle** ['dɔːdᵊl] to do things of no importance without haste – 23 **ennui** ['ɑːnwiː] *(Fr)* extreme boredom – 30 **miscellaneous** [ˌmɪsᵊl'eɪnɪəs] various, assorted

letters and other papers, with one or two musical instruments and a few books. Here, however, after a long and very deliberate scrutiny, I saw nothing to excite particular suspicion.

"At length my eyes, in going the circuit of the room, fell upon
5 a trumpery filigree card-rack of pasteboard, that hung dangling by a dirty blue ribbon from a little brass knob just beneath the middle of the mantelpiece. In this rack, which had three or four compartments, were five or six visiting cards and a solitary letter. This last was much soiled and crumpled. It was torn nearly in
10 two, across the middle – as if a design, in the first instance, to tear it entirely up as worthless, had been altered, or stayed, in the second. It had a large black seal, bearing the D– cipher very conspicuously, and was addressed, in a diminutive female hand, to D– , the minister, himself. It was thrust carelessly, and even,
15 as it seemed, contemptuously, into one of the upper divisions of the rack.

"No sooner had I glanced at this letter, than I concluded it to be that of which I was in search. To be sure, it was, to all appearance, radically different from the one of which the Prefect
20 had read us so minute a description. Here the seal was large and black, with the D– cipher; there it was small and red, with the ducal arms of the S– family. Here, the address, to the Minister, was diminutive and feminine; there the superscription, to a certain royal personage, was markedly bold and decided; the
25 size alone formed a point of correspondence. But then, the radicalness of these differences, which was excessive; the dirt, the soiled and torn condition of the paper, so inconsistent with the true methodical habits of D– , and so suggestive of a design to delude the beholder into an idea of the worthlessness of the
30 document; these things, together with the hyperobtrusive situation of this document, full in the view of every visitor, and

---

5 **trumpery** *(adj, old)* worthless – 5 **filigree** extravagant – 5 **pasteboard** cardboard –
12 **cipher** ['saɪfəʳ] *(old) here:* signature – 13 **conspicuously** clearly, visibly – 13 **in a
diminutive hand** in very small handwriting – 22 **ducal** of a duke – 22 (coat of) **arms**
Wappen – 30 **hyperobtrusive** *(old)* too obvious

thus exactly in accordance with the conclusions to which I had previously arrived; these things, I say, were strongly corroborative of suspicion, in one who came with the intention to suspect.

"I protracted my visit as long as possible, and, while I
5 maintained a most animated discussion with the Minister, on a topic which I knew well had never failed to interest and excite him, I kept my attention really riveted upon the letter. In this examination, I committed to memory its external appearance and arrangement in the rack, and also fell, at length, upon a
10 discovery which set at rest whatever trivial doubt I might have entertained. In scrutinizing the edges of the paper, I observed them to be more chafed than seemed necessary. They presented the broken appearance which is manifested when a stiff paper, having been once folded and pressed with a folder, is refolded
15 in a reversed direction, in the same creases or edges which had formed the original fold. This discovery was sufficient. It was clear to me that the letter had been turned, as a glove, inside out, re-directed, and re-sealed. I bade the Minister good morning, and took my departure at once, leaving a gold snuff-box upon
20 the table.

"The next morning I called for the snuff-box, when we resumed, quite eagerly, the conversation of the preceding day. While thus engaged, however, a loud report, as if of a pistol, was heard immediately beneath the windows of the hotel, and was
25 succeeded by a series of fearful screams, and the shoutings of a mob. D– rushed to a casement, threw it open, and looked out. In the meantime, I stepped to the card-rack, took the letter, put it in my pocket, and replaced it by a fac-simile, (so far as regards externals), which I had carefully prepared at my lodgings;
30 imitating the D– cipher, very readily, by means of a seal formed of bread.

---

2 **to be corroborative** [kəˈrɒbᵊrətɪv] **of sth** to confirm sth – 4 **to protract** to prolong –
7 **riveted** firmly fixed – 12 **chafed** worn, damaged – 23 **report** *here:* banging sound, *usu*
of a gunshot – 28 **fac-simile** *(Lat)* copy

"The disturbance in the street had been occasioned by the frantic behavior of a man with a musket. He had fired it among a crowd of women and children. It proved, however, to have been without ball, and the fellow was suffered to go his way as a lunatic or a drunkard. When he had gone, D– came from the window, whither I had followed him immediately upon securing the object in view. Soon afterwards I bade him farewell. The pretended lunatic was a man in my own pay.

"But what purpose had you," I asked, "in replacing the letter by a fac-simile? Would it not have been better, at the first visit, to have seized it openly, and departed?"

"D– ," replied Dupin, "is a desperate man, and a man of nerve. His hotel, too, is not without attendants devoted to his interests. Had I made the wild attempt you suggest, I might never have left the Ministerial presence alive. The good people of Paris might have heard of me no more. But I had an object apart from these considerations. You know my political prepossessions. In this matter, I act as a partisan of the lady concerned. For eighteen months the Minister has had her in his power. She has now him in hers; since, being unaware that the letter is not in his possession, he will proceed with his exactions as if it was. Thus will he inevitably commit himself, at once, to his political destruction. His downfall, too, will not be more precipitate than awkward. It is all very well to talk about the facilis descensus Averni, but in all kinds of climbing, as Catalani said of singing, it is far more easy to get up than to come down. In the present instance I have no sympathy – at least no pity – for him who descends. He is the monstrum horrendum, an unprincipled man of genius. I confess, however, that I should like very well to know the precise character of his thoughts, when, being defied

5 **lunatic** mentally ill person – 17 **prepossessions** bias *(Voreingenommenheit)* –
18 **partisan** supporter – 21 **exactions** demands – 23 **precipitate** quick, fast – 24 **facilis descensus Averni** *(Lat)* quote from Virgil's *Aeneid* expressing how easy it is to descend to the underworld – 25 Alfredo **Catalani** (1854–1893) Italian operatic composer –
28 **monstrum horrendum** *(Lat)* a horrific monster (from Virgil's *Aeneid*)

by her whom the Prefect terms 'a certain personage,' he is reduced to opening the letter which I left for him in the card-rack."

"How? Did you put any thing particular in it?"

5   "Why – it did not seem altogether right to leave the interior blank – that would have been insulting. D– , at Vienna once, did me an evil turn, which I told him, quite good-humoredly, that I should remember. So, as I knew he would feel some curiosity in regard to the identity of the person who had outwitted him,

10   I thought it a pity not to give him a clue. He is well acquainted with my MS., and I just copied into the middle of the blank sheet the words:

Un dessein si funeste, S'il n'est digne d'Atree, est digne de Thyeste.

15   They are to be found in Crebillon's 'Atree.'"

9 **to outwit sb** to trick sb (by being cleverer than them) – 11 **MS.** *(abb)* "manuscript" (old-fashioned word for "handwriting") *(Handschrift)* – 13 **"Un dessein si funeste, S'il n'est digne d'Atree, est digne de Thyeste."** "If such a sinister design isn't worthy of Atreus, it is worthy of Thyestes." (quote from Crébillon's play *Atree et Thyeste* (1707) about the Greek mythological twin brothers Atreus and Thyestes who murdered their half-brother Chrysippus in their desire for power) – 15 Prosper Jolyot **Crébillon** (1674–1762) French poet and playwright

Sir Arthur Conan Doyle (1859–1930)

Arthur Conan Doyle (right) was born in 1859. "Conan" was actually his middle, not his surname, which was just "Doyle". Knighted in 1902, he will always be remembered for creating the eccentric detective, Sherlock Holmes, and his assistant and biographer, Dr. John Watson. But he was also a poet, playwright and author of historical and science fiction.

In 1886, Sherlock Holmes made his first appearance, in the novel *A Study in Scarlet*, but fame and success only truly came in 1891 with *The Adventures of Sherlock Holmes*, the first series of short stories, printed in *The Strand Magazine* and starting with *A Scandal in Bohemia*. By 1927, four novels and 56 short stories about the consultant detective and his co-resident (at 221B, Baker Street) and friend, Watson, had been published. Doyle was even forced to revive Holmes by popular demand, despite the fact that he had been "killed off" in *The Final Problem* in 1893.

Today, Sherlock Holmes is still one of the world's best known fictional detectives. His cases have been made into films, radio and stage plays, video games and even apps.

His equally famous creator, Sir Arthur Conan Doyle, influenced not only today's popular culture but also future generations of crime writers, and his role in the development of the literary genre of detective fiction is perhaps unparalled throughout the world.

Doyle died in 1930 of heart failure in Crowborough, Sussex.

Story 3: A Study in Scarlet (1886)

by Sir Arthur Conan Doyle

Chapter 1

In the year 1878 I took my degree of Doctor of Medicine of
5 the University of London, and proceeded to Netley to go
through the course prescribed for surgeons in the army. Having
completed my studies there, I was duly attached to the Fifth
Northumberland Fusiliers as Assistant Surgeon. The regiment
was stationed in India at the time, and before I could join it, the
10 second Afghan war had broken out. On landing at Bombay, I
learned that my corps had advanced through the passes, and
was already deep in the enemy's country. I followed, however,
with many other officers who were in the same situation as
myself, and succeeded in reaching Candahar in safety, where I
15 found my regiment, and at once entered upon my new duties.

The campaign brought honours and promotion to many, but
for me it had nothing but misfortune and disaster. I was removed
from my brigade and attached to the Berkshires, with whom I
served at the fatal battle of Maiwand. There I was struck on the
20 shoulder by a Jezail bullet, which shattered the bone and grazed
the subclavian artery. I should have fallen into the hands of the
murderous Ghazis had it not been for the devotion and courage
shown by Murray, my orderly, who threw me across a pack-horse,
and succeeded in bringing me safely to the British lines.

25 Worn with pain, and weak from the prolonged hardships which
I had undergone, I was removed, with a great train of wounded

---

5 **Netley** village in southern England and at that time the site of the huge Royal
Victoria Military Hospital – 7 **duly** straightaway – 7 **to be attached to** *(military)* to be
assigned to – 10 **second** Anglo-**Afghan war** fought between the United Kingdom and
the Emirate of Afghanistan from 1878 to 1880 – 20 **Jezail** Afghan rifle – 20 **to graze sth**
etw. streifen – 21 **subclavian artery** main artery leading to the throat and the arm –
22 **Ghazi** *here*: Afghan warrior – 23 **orderly** hospital attendant

sufferers, to the base hospital at Peshawar. Here I rallied, and had already improved so far as to be able to walk about the wards, and even to bask a little upon the verandah, when I was struck down by enteric fever, that curse of our Indian
5   possessions. For months my life was despaired of, and when at last I came to myself and became convalescent, I was so weak and emaciated that a medical board determined that not a day should be lost in sending me back to England. I was dispatched, accordingly, in the troopship "Orontes," and landed a month
10   later on Portsmouth jetty, with my health irretrievably ruined, but with permission from a paternal government to spend the next nine months in attempting to improve it.

I had neither kith nor kin in England, and was therefore as free as air – or as free as an income of eleven shillings and
15   sixpence a day will permit a man to be. Under such circumstances, I naturally gravitated to London, that great cesspool into which all the loungers and idlers of the Empire are irresistibly drained. There I stayed for some time at a private hotel in the Strand, leading a comfortless, meaningless existence, and spending such
20   money as I had, considerably more freely than I ought. So alarming did the state of my finances become, that I soon realized that I must either leave the metropolis and rusticate somewhere in the country, or that I must make a complete alteration in my style of living. Choosing the latter alternative, I began by making
25   up my mind to leave the hotel, and to take up my quarters in some less pretentious and less expensive domicile.

On the very day that I had come to this conclusion, I was standing at the Criterion Bar, when some one tapped me on the

1 **Peshawar** city (now) in the north of Pakistan (Until 1947 it was in India, which was part of the British Empire.) – 1 **to rally** to recover – 3 **to bask** to sit in relaxation in the sun – 4 **enteric fever** inflammation of the stomach and intestines – 6 **convalescent** [ˌkɒnvəˈlesᵊnt] improved in health – 7 **emaciated** very thin – 10 **jetty** pier – 13 **neither kith nor kin** no close family members, relatives – 16 **cesspool** *Jauchegrube* – 17 **loungers and idlers** lazy people – 18 **the Strand** well-known and at that time (1855–1900) fashionable local district within the metropolitan area of London. Today it is a major street in the City of Westminster. – 22 **to rusticate** to go into exile

shoulder, and turning round I recognized young Stamford, who had been a dresser under me at Barts. The sight of a friendly face in the great wilderness of London is a pleasant thing indeed to a lonely man. In old days Stamford had never been a particular
5 crony of mine, but now I hailed him with enthusiasm, and he, in his turn, appeared to be delighted to see me. In the exuberance of my joy, I asked him to lunch with me at the Holborn, and we started off together in a hansom.

"Whatever have you been doing with yourself, Watson?" he
10 asked in undisguised wonder, as we rattled through the crowded London streets. "You are as thin as a lath and as brown as a nut."

I gave him a short sketch of my adventures, and had hardly concluded it by the time that we reached our destination.
15 "Poor devil!" he said, commiseratingly, after he had listened to my misfortunes. "What are you up to now?"

"Looking for lodgings." I answered. "Trying to solve the problem as to whether it is possible to get comfortable rooms at a reasonable price."
20 "That's a strange thing," remarked my companion; "you are the second man to-day that has used that expression to me."

"And who was the first?" I asked.

"A fellow who is working at the chemical laboratory up at the hospital. He was bemoaning himself this morning because he
25 could not get someone to go halves with him in some nice rooms which he had found, and which were too much for his purse."

"By Jove!" I cried, "If he really wants someone to share the rooms and the expense, I am the very man for him. I should prefer having a partner to being alone."

---

2 **dresser** doctor's assistant – 2 **Barts** *(abb)* St Bartholomew's Hospital, London –
5 **crony** *(inf, sl)* friend – 5 **to hail sb** to greet sb – 6 **exuberance** [ɪgˈzjuːbərᵊnts]
enthusiasm, excitement – 8 **hansom** horse-drawn carriage *(usu* a taxi*)* – 11 **lath** *(old)*
thin strip of wood – 15 **commiserating** empathising – 24 **to bemoan** *(fml)* to regret
things and complain about one's fate – 25 **to go halves with sb** to share fifty-fifty –
27 **By Jove!** *(old) Donnerwetter!*

Young Stamford looked rather strangely at me over his wine-glass. "You don't know Sherlock Holmes yet," he said, "perhaps you would not care for him as a constant companion."

"Why, what is there against him?"

5 "Oh, I didn't say there was anything against him. He is a little queer in his ideas – an enthusiast in some branches of science. As far as I know he is a decent fellow enough."

"A medical student, I suppose?" said I.

"No – I have no idea what he intends to go in for. I believe he
10 is well up in anatomy, and he is a first-class chemist; but, as far as I know, he has never taken out any systematic medical classes. His studies are very desultory and eccentric, but he has amassed a lot of out-of-the way knowledge which would astonish his professors."

15 "Did you never ask him what he was going in for?" I asked.

"No; he is not a man that it is easy to draw out, though he can be communicative enough when the fancy seizes him."

"I should like to meet him," I said. "If I am to lodge with anyone, I should prefer a man of studious and quiet habits. I
20 am not strong enough yet to stand much noise or excitement. I had enough of both in Afghanistan to last me for the remainder of my natural existence. How could I meet this friend of yours?"

"He is sure to be at the laboratory," returned my companion.
25 "He either avoids the place for weeks, or else he works there from morning to night. If you like, we shall drive round together after luncheon."

"Certainly," I answered, and the conversation drifted away into other channels.

30 As we made our way to the hospital after leaving the Holborn, Stamford gave me a few more particulars about the gentleman whom I proposed to take as a fellow-lodger.

"You mustn't blame me if you don't get on with him," he said; "I know nothing more of him than I have learned from meeting

12 **desultory** half-hearted

him occasionally in the laboratory. You proposed this arrangement, so you must not hold me responsible."

"If we don't get on it will be easy to part company," I answered. "It seems to me, Stamford," I added, looking hard at my
5 companion, "that you have some reason for washing your hands of the matter. Is this fellow's temper so formidable, or what is it? Don't be mealy-mouthed about it."

"It is not easy to express the inexpressible," he answered with a laugh. "Holmes is a little too scientific for my tastes – it
10 approaches to cold-bloodedness. I could imagine his giving a friend a little pinch of the latest vegetable alkaloid, not out of malevolence, you understand, but simply out of a spirit of inquiry in order to have an accurate idea of the effects. To do him justice, I think that he would take it himself with the same
15 readiness. He appears to have a passion for definite and exact knowledge."

"Very right too."

"Yes, but it may be pushed to excess. When it comes to beating the subjects in the dissecting-rooms with a stick, it is certainly
20 taking rather a bizarre shape."

"Beating the subjects!"

"Yes, to verify how far bruises may be produced after death. I saw him at it with my own eyes."

"And yet you say he is not a medical student?"

25 "No. Heaven knows what the objects of his studies are. But here we are, and you must form your own impressions about him." As he spoke, we turned down a narrow lane and passed through a small side-door, which opened into a wing of the great hospital. It was familiar ground to me, and I needed no guiding
30 as we ascended the bleak stone staircase and made our way down the long corridor with its vista of whitewashed wall and

---

7 **to be mealy-mouthed** *(old)* to make excuses – 11 **pinch** small quantity – 11 **alkaloid** naturally occuring chemical compound – 12 **malevolence** [məˈlevələnts] ill will, bad intentions

dun-coloured doors. Near the further end a low arched passage branched away from it and led to the chemical laboratory.

This was a lofty chamber, lined and littered with countless bottles. Broad, low tables were scattered about, which bristled
5 with retorts, test-tubes, and little Bunsen lamps, with their blue flickering flames. There was only one student in the room, who was bending over a distant table absorbed in his work. At the sound of our steps he glanced round and sprang to his feet with a cry of pleasure. "I've found it! I've found it," he shouted to my
10 companion, running towards us with a test-tube in his hand. "I have found a re-agent which is precipitated by hoemoglobin, and by nothing else." Had he discovered a gold mine, greater delight could not have shone upon his features.

"Dr. Watson, Mr. Sherlock Holmes," said Stamford, introducing
15 us.

"How are you?" he said cordially, gripping my hand with a strength for which I should hardly have given him credit. "You have been in Afghanistan, I perceive."

"How on earth did you know that?" I asked in astonish-
20 ment.

"Never mind," said he, chuckling to himself. "The question now is about hoemoglobin. No doubt you see the significance of this discovery of mine?"

"It is interesting, chemically, no doubt," I answered, "but
25 practically–"

"Why, man, it is the most practical medico-legal discovery for years. Don't you see that it gives us an infallible test for blood stains. Come over here now!" He seized me by the coat-sleeve in his eagerness, and drew me over to the table at which he had
30 been working. "Let us have some fresh blood," he said, digging a long bodkin into his finger, and drawing off the resulting drop of blood in a chemical pipette. "Now, I add this small quantity

11 **re-agent** substance added to a system to cause a chemical reaction – 11 **to precipitate** [prɪˈsɪpɪteɪt] to trigger – 16 **cordially** in a friendly way – 27 **infallible** reliable, without error – 31 **bodkin** long needle

of blood to a litre of water. You perceive that the resulting mixture has the appearance of pure water. The proportion of blood cannot be more than one in a million. I have no doubt, however, that we shall be able to obtain the characteristic reaction." As

5 he spoke, he threw into the vessel a few white crystals, and then added some drops of a transparent fluid. In an instant the contents assumed a dull mahogany colour, and a brownish dust was precipitated to the bottom of the glass jar.

"Ha! ha!" he cried, clapping his hands, and looking as delighted

10 as a child with a new toy. "What do you think of that?"

"It seems to be a very delicate test," I remarked.

"Beautiful! Beautiful! The old Guiacum test was very clumsy and uncertain. So is the microscopic examination for blood corpuscles. The latter is valueless if the stains are a few

15 hours old. Now, this appears to act as well whether the blood is old or new. Had this test been invented, there are hundreds of men now walking the earth who would long ago have paid the penalty of their crimes."

"Indeed!" I murmured.

20 "Criminal cases are continually hinging upon that one point. A man is suspected of a crime months perhaps after it has been committed. His linen or clothes are examined, and brownish stains discovered upon them. Are they blood stains, or mud stains, or rust stains, or fruit stains, or what are they? That is a

25 question which has puzzled many an expert, and why? Because there was no reliable test. Now we have the Sherlock Holmes test, and there will no longer be any difficulty."

His eyes fairly glittered as he spoke, and he put his hand over his heart and bowed as if to some applauding crowd conjured

30 up by his imagination.

"You are to be congratulated," I remarked, considerably surprised at his enthusiasm.

---

12 **Guiacum test** method to detect the presence of invisible blood in the faeces (*Fäkalien*) – 14 **corpuscle** ['kɔːpʌsᵊl] blood cell

"There was the case of Von Bischoff at Frankfort last year. He would certainly have been hung had this test been in existence. Then there was Mason of Bradford, and the notorious Muller, and Lefevre of Montpellier, and Samson of New Orleans. I could name a score of cases in which it would have been decisive."

"You seem to be a walking calendar of crime," said Stamford with a laugh. "You might start a paper on those lines. Call it the 'Police News of the Past.'"

"Very interesting reading it might be made, too," remarked Sherlock Holmes, sticking a small piece of plaster over the prick on his finger. "I have to be careful," he continued, turning to me with a smile, "for I dabble with poisons a good deal." He held out his hand as he spoke, and I noticed that it was all mottled over with similar pieces of plaster, and discoloured with strong acids.

"We came here on business," said Stamford, sitting down on a high three-legged stool, and pushing another one in my direction with his foot. "My friend here wants to take diggings, and as you were complaining that you could get no one to go halves with you, I thought that I had better bring you together."

Sherlock Holmes seemed delighted at the idea of sharing his rooms with me. "I have my eye on a suite in Baker Street," he said, "which would suit us down to the ground. You don't mind the smell of strong tobacco, I hope?"

"I always smoke 'ship's' myself," I answered.

"That's good enough. I generally have chemicals about, and occasionally do experiments. Would that annoy you?"

"By no means."

"Let me see – what are my other shortcomings. I get in the dumps at times, and don't open my mouth for days on end. You

---

12 **to dabble with sth** to work with sth on the side – 13 **mottled** flecked, streaked – 18 **to take diggings** *(old, sl)* to find lodgings, to move – 26 **ship's** particular way of preparing tobacco by sailors on board British military ships – 30 **to get in the dumps** *(inf)* to feel depressed

must not think I am sulky when I do that. Just let me alone, and I'll soon be right. What have you to confess now? It's just as well for two fellows to know the worst of one another before they begin to live together."

5 I laughed at this cross-examination. "I keep a bull pup," I said, "and I object to rows because my nerves are shaken, and I get up at all sorts of ungodly hours, and I am extremely lazy. I have another set of vices when I'm well, but those are the principal ones at present."

10 "Do you include violin-playing in your category of rows?" he asked, anxiously.

"It depends on the player," I answered. "A well-played violin is a treat for the gods – a badly-played one –"

"Oh, that's all right," he cried, with a merry laugh. "I think we 15 may consider the thing as settled – that is, if the rooms are agreeable to you."

"When shall we see them?"

"Call for me here at noon to-morrow, and we'll go together and settle everything," he answered.

20 "All right – noon exactly," said I, shaking his hand.

We left him working among his chemicals, and we walked together towards my hotel.

"By the way," I asked suddenly, stopping and turning upon Stamford, "how the deuce did he know that I had come from 25 Afghanistan?"

My companion smiled an enigmatical smile. "That's just his little peculiarity," he said. "A good many people have wanted to know how he finds things out."

"Oh! A mystery is it?" I cried, rubbing my hands. "This is very 30 piquant. I am much obliged to you for bringing us together. 'The proper study of mankind is man,' you know."

---

1 **sulky** moody, brooding – 6 **row** [raʊ] *(BE)* argument – 8 **vice** moral weakness –
27 **peculiarity** [pɪˌkjuːliˈærəti] strange habit – 30 **piquant** [ˈpiːkənt] fascinating

"You must study him, then," Stamford said, as he bade me good-bye. "You'll find him a knotty problem, though. I'll wager he learns more about you than you about him. Good-bye."

"Good-bye," I answered, and strolled on to my hotel, considerably interested in my new acquaintance.

Chapter 2. The Science of Deduction

We met next day as he had arranged, and inspected the rooms at No. 221B, Baker Street, of which he had spoken at our meeting. They consisted of a couple of comfortable bedrooms and a single large airy sitting-room, cheerfully furnished, and illuminated by two broad windows. So desirable in every way were the apartments, and so moderate did the terms seem when divided between us, that the bargain was concluded upon the spot, and we at once entered into possession. That very evening I moved my things round from the hotel, and on the following morning Sherlock Holmes followed me with several boxes and portmanteaus. For a day or two we were busily employed in unpacking and laying out our property to the best advantage. That done, we gradually began to settle down and to accommodate ourselves to our new surroundings.

Holmes was certainly not a difficult man to live with. He was quiet in his ways, and his habits were regular. It was rare for him to be up after ten at night, and he had invariably breakfasted and gone out before I rose in the morning. Sometimes he spent his day at the chemical laboratory, sometimes in the dissecting-rooms, and occasionally in long walks, which appeared to take him into the lowest portions of the City. Nothing could exceed his energy when the working fit was upon him; but now and again a reaction would seize him, and for days on end he would

---

1 **to bid [bade, bidden] sb goodbye** to say goodbye to sb – 2 **to wager** to bet – 14 **to enter into possession** *here:* to buy the apartment – 17 **portmanteau** [pɔːˈmætəʊ] *(old)* large suitcase – 20 **to accommodate oneself to sth** to get used to sth – 27 **to exceed** to surpass, be bigger than

lie upon the sofa in the sitting-room, hardly uttering a word or moving a muscle from morning to night. On these occasions I have noticed such a dreamy, vacant expression in his eyes, that I might have suspected him of being addicted to the use of some narcotic, had not the temperance and cleanliness of his whole life forbidden such a notion.

As the weeks went by, my interest in him and my curiosity as to his aims in life gradually deepened and increased. His very person and appearance were such as to strike the attention of the most casual observer. In height he was rather over six feet, and so excessively lean that he seemed to be considerably taller. His eyes were sharp and piercing, save during those intervals of torpor to which I have alluded; and his thin, hawk-like nose gave his whole expression an air of alertness and decision. His chin, too, had the prominence and squareness which mark the man of determination. His hands were invariably blotted with ink and stained with chemicals, yet he was possessed of extraordinary delicacy of touch, as I frequently had occasion to observe when I watched him manipulating his fragile philosophical instruments.

The reader may set me down as a hopeless busybody, when I confess how much this man stimulated my curiosity, and how often I endeavoured to break through the reticence which he showed on all that concerned himself. Before pronouncing judgment, however, be it remembered, how objectless was my life, and how little there was to engage my attention. My health forbade me from venturing out unless the weather was exceptionally genial, and I had no friends who would call upon me and break the monotony of my daily existence. Under these circumstances, I eagerly hailed the little mystery which hung around my companion, and spent much of my time in endeavouring to unravel it.

---

3 **vacant** empty – 11 **lean** thin – 13 **torpor** lethargy – 14 **alertness** watchfulness – 19 **to manipulate** to handle carefully – 23 **to endeavour** [ɪnˈdevəʳ] to try hard – 23 **reticence** [ˈretɪsᵊnts] reserve, coolness of manner – 32 **to unravel sth** to solve a mystery

He was not studying medicine. He had himself, in reply to a question, confirmed Stamford's opinion upon that point. Neither did he appear to have pursued any course of reading which might fit him for a degree in science or any other recognized
5 portal which would give him an entrance into the learned world. Yet his zeal for certain studies was remarkable, and within eccentric limits his knowledge was so extraordinarily ample and minute that his observations have fairly astounded me. Surely no man would work so hard or attain such precise information
10 unless he had some definite end in view. Desultory readers are seldom remarkable for the exactness of their learning. No man burdens his mind with small matters unless he has some very good reason for doing so.

His ignorance was as remarkable as his knowledge. Of
15 contemporary literature, philosophy and politics he appeared to know next to nothing. Upon my quoting Thomas Carlyle, he inquired in the naivest way who he might be and what he had done. My surprise reached a climax, however, when I found incidentally that he was ignorant of the Copernican Theory and
20 of the composition of the Solar System. That any civilized human being in this nineteenth century should not be aware that the earth travelled round the sun appeared to be to me such an extraordinary fact that I could hardly realize it.

"You appear to be astonished," he said, smiling at my
25 expression of surprise. "Now that I do know it I shall do my best to forget it."

"To forget it!"

"You see," he explained, "I consider that a man's brain originally is like a little empty attic, and you have to stock it with such
30 furniture as you choose. A fool takes in all the lumber of every sort that he comes across, so that the knowledge which might

6 **zeal** enthusiasm – 8 **to astound** to surprise greatly – 11 **seldom** rarely – 16 **Thomas Carlyle** (1795–1881) Scottish philosopher and historian – 17 **to inquire** to ask – 19 **Copernican Theory** astronomical model created by Nicolaus Copernicus in 1543 according to which the sun is the motionless centre of our universe with the planets rotating around it – 30 **lumber** *(sl, old)* junk

be useful to him gets crowded out, or at best is jumbled up with a lot of other things so that he has a difficulty in laying his hands upon it. Now the skilful workman is very careful indeed as to what he takes into his brain-attic. He will have nothing but the
5 tools which may help him in doing his work, but of these he has a large assortment, and all in the most perfect order. It is a mistake to think that that little room has elastic walls and can distend to any extent. Depend upon it there comes a time when for every addition of knowledge you forget something that you
10 knew before. It is of the highest importance, therefore, not to have useless facts elbowing out the useful ones."

"But the Solar System!" I protested.

"What the deuce is it to me?" he interrupted impatiently. "You say that we go round the sun. If we went round the moon it
15 would not make a pennyworth of difference to me or to my work."

I was on the point of asking him what that work might be, but something in his manner showed me that the question would be an unwelcome one. I pondered over our short conversation,
20 however, and endeavoured to draw my deductions from it. He said that he would acquire no knowledge which did not bear upon his object. Therefore all the knowledge which he possessed was such as would be useful to him. I enumerated in my own mind all the various points upon which he had shown me that
25 he was exceptionally well-informed. I even took a pencil and jotted them down. I could not help smiling at the document when I had completed it. It ran in this way:

SHERLOCK HOLMES – his limits
1. Knowledge of Literature – Nil.
30 2. Philosophy – Nil.
3. Astronomy – Nil.

---

1 **to be jumbled up** to be in chaos – 8 **to distend** *sich aufblähen* – 14 **to not make a pennyworth of difference** to make no difference at all – 19 **to ponder (over) sth** to consider sth very carefully – 29 **nil** nothing

4. Politics – Feeble.
5. Botany – Variable. Well up in belladonna, opium, and poisons generally. Knows nothing of practical gardening.
6. Geology – Practical, but limited. Tells at a glance different soils from each other. After walks has shown me splashes upon his trousers, and told me by their colour and consistence in what part of London he had received them.
7. Chemistry – Profound.
8. Anatomy – Accurate, but unsystematic.
9. Sensational Literature – Immense. He appears to know every detail of every horror perpetrated in the century.
10. Plays the violin well.
11. Is an expert singlestick player, boxer, and swordsman.
12. Has a good practical knowledge of British law.

When I had got so far in my list I threw it into the fire in despair. "If I can only find what the fellow is driving at by reconciling all these accomplishments, and discovering a calling which needs them all," I said to myself, "I may as well give up the attempt at once."

I see that I have alluded above to his powers upon the violin. These were very remarkable, but as eccentric as all his other accomplishments. That he could play pieces, and difficult pieces, I knew well, because at my request he has played me some of Mendelssohn's Lieder, and other favourites. When left to himself, however, he would seldom produce any music or attempt any recognized air. Leaning back in his arm-chair of an evening, he would close his eyes and scrape carelessly at the fiddle which was thrown across his knee. Sometimes the chords were sonorous and melancholy. Occasionally they were fantastic and cheerful.

1 **feeble** weak – 2 **belladonna** extremely toxic plant, historically used as a medicine, cosmetic, poison and drug – 5 **soil** *here:* types of earth – 11 **perpetrated** committed – 13 **singlestick** type of martial arts, performed with a round, wooden club – 16 **to be driving at sth** *auf etw hinauswollen* – 16 **to reconcile** to combine – 26 **air** melody – 28 **sonorous** deep and rich (sound)

Clearly they reflected the thoughts which possessed him, but whether the music aided those thoughts, or whether the playing was simply the result of a whim or fancy was more than I could determine. I might have rebelled against these exasperating
5 solos had it not been that he usually terminated them by playing in quick succession a whole series of my favourite airs as a slight compensation for the trial upon my patience.

During the first week or so we had no callers, and I had begun to think that my companion was as friendless a man as I was
10 myself. Presently, however, I found that he had many acquaintances, and those in the most different classes of society. There was one little sallow rat-faced, dark-eyed fellow who was introduced to me as Mr. Lestrade, and who came three or four times in a single week. One morning a young girl called,
15 fashionably dressed, and stayed for half an hour or more. The same afternoon brought a grey-headed, seedy visitor, looking like a Jew pedlar, who appeared to me to be much excited, and who was closely followed by a slip-shod elderly woman. On another occasion an old white-haired gentleman had an
20 interview with my companion; and on another a railway porter in his velveteen uniform. When any of these nondescript individuals put in an appearance, Sherlock Holmes used to beg for the use of the sitting-room, and I would retire to my bedroom. He always apologized to me for putting me to this
25 inconvenience.

"I have to use this room as a place of business," he said, "and these people are my clients."

Again I had an opportunity of asking him a point blank question, and again my delicacy prevented me from forcing

---

3 **whim** random idea or mood – 4 **exasperating** [ɪgzˈæspʰreɪtɪŋ] very irritating –
7 **compensation** recompense *(Entschädigung)* – 7 **trial** test – 8 **callers** visitors –
12 **sallow** pale – 16 **seedy** dirty and dubious – 17 **pedlar** *(old)* travelling salesman –
18 **slip-shod** ragged, untidily dressed – 20 **porter** baggage carrier – 21 **velveteen**
Veloursamt – 23 **to retire** to withdraw – 28 **point blank** blunt, direct – 29 **delicacy**
discretion

another man to confide in me. I imagined at the time that he had some strong reason for not alluding to it, but he soon dispelled the idea by coming round to the subject of his own accord.

5   It was upon the 4th of March, as I have good reason to remember, that I rose somewhat earlier than usual, and found that Sherlock Holmes had not yet finished his breakfast. The landlady had become so accustomed to my late habits that my place had not been laid nor my coffee prepared. With the 10 unreasonable petulance of mankind I rang the bell and gave a curt intimation that I was ready. Then I picked up a magazine from the table and attempted to while away the time with it, while my companion munched silently at his toast. One of the articles had a pencil mark at the heading, and I naturally began 15 to run my eye through it.

    Its somewhat ambitious title was "The Book of Life," and it attempted to show how much an observant man might learn by an accurate and systematic examination of all that came in his way. It struck me as being a remarkable mixture of shrewdness 20 and of absurdity. The reasoning was close and intense, but the deductions appeared to me to be far-fetched and exaggerated. The writer claimed by a momentary expression, a twitch of a muscle or a glance of an eye, to fathom a man's inmost thoughts. Deceit, according to him, was an impossibility in the case of 25 one trained to observation and analysis. His conclusions were as infallible as so many propositions of Euclid. So startling would his results appear to the uninitiated that until they learned the processes by which he had arrived at them they might well consider him as a necromancer.

---

10 **petulance** ['petʃələnts] child-like annoyance – 11 **curt** abrupt, rude – 11 **intimation** announcement – 19 **shrewdness** cleverness – 20 **reasoning** logical thinking – 23 **to fathom** to understand – 24 **deceit** trickery, fraud *(Betrug)* – 26 **Euclid** ['juːklɪd] (ca. 300 BC) Greek mathematician – 27 **the uninitiated** an uninstructed person, amateur – 29 **necromancer** magician capable of communicating with the dead

"From a drop of water," said the writer, "a logician could infer the possibility of an Atlantic or a Niagara without having seen or heard of one or the other. So all life is a great chain, the nature of which is known whenever we are shown a single link of it.
5 Like all other arts, the Science of Deduction and Analysis is one which can only be acquired by long and patient study nor is life long enough to allow any mortal to attain the highest possible perfection in it. Before turning to those moral and mental aspects of the matter which present the greatest difficulties, let the
10 enquirer begin by mastering more elementary problems. Let him, on meeting a fellow-mortal, learn at a glance to distinguish the history of the man, and the trade or profession to which he belongs. Puerile as such an exercise may seem, it sharpens the faculties of observation, and teaches one where to look and what
15 to look for. By a man's finger nails, by his coat-sleeve, by his boot, by his trouser knees, by the callosities of his forefinger and thumb, by his expression, by his shirt cuffs – by each of these things a man's calling is plainly revealed. That all united should fail to enlighten the competent enquirer in any case is almost
20 inconceivable."

"What ineffable twaddle!" I cried, slapping the magazine down on the table, "I never read such rubbish in my life."

"What is it?" asked Sherlock Holmes.

"Why, this article," I said, pointing at it with my egg spoon as
25 I sat down to my breakfast. "I see that you have read it since you have marked it. I don't deny that it is smartly written. It irritates me though. It is evidently the theory of some arm-chair lounger who evolves all these neat little paradoxes in the seclusion of his own study. It is not practical. I should like to see him clapped
30 down in a third class carriage on the Underground, and asked

---

13 **puerile** ['pjʊəraɪl] childish – 14 **faculties** natural abilities – 16 **callosity** *Hornhautbildung* – 20 **inconceivable** unimaginable – 21 **ineffable** inexpressible – 21 **twaddle** ['twɒdəl] *(sl)* nonsense – 28 **to evolve** to develop, to create – 28 **seclusion** privacy – 29 **study** office

to give the trades of all his fellow-travellers. I would lay a thousand to one against him."

"You would lose your money," Sherlock Holmes remarked calmly. "As for the article I wrote it myself."

5 "You!"

"Yes, I have a turn both for observation and for deduction. The theories which I have expressed there, and which appear to you to be so chimerical are really extremely practical – so practical that I depend upon them for my bread and cheese."

10 "And how?" I asked involuntarily.

"Well, I have a trade of my own. I suppose I am the only one in the world. I'm a consulting detective, if you can understand what that is. Here in London we have lots of Government detectives and lots of private ones. When these fellows are at 15 fault they come to me, and I manage to put them on the right scent. They lay all the evidence before me, and I am generally able, by the help of my knowledge of the history of crime, to set them straight. There is a strong family resemblance about misdeeds, and if you have all the details of a thousand at your 20 finger ends, it is odd if you can't unravel the thousand and first. Lestrade is a well-known detective. He got himself into a fog recently over a forgery case, and that was what brought him here."

"And these other people?"

25 "They are mostly sent on by private inquiry agencies. They are all people who are in trouble about something, and want a little enlightening. I listen to their story, they listen to my comments, and then I pocket my fee."

"But do you mean to say," I said, "that without leaving your 30 room you can unravel some knot which other men can make nothing of, although they have seen every detail for themselves?"

---

8 **chimerical** [kaɪˈmerɪkᵊl] absurd – 14 **to be at fault** *here:* not to know what else to do – 22 **forgery** [ˈfɔːdʒᵊri] crime of imitating objects or documents with the intent to deceive or to earn profit by selling the forged item

"Quite so. I have a kind of intuition that way. Now and again a case turns up which is a little more complex. Then I have to bustle about and see things with my own eyes. You see I have a lot of special knowledge which I apply to the problem, and which
5 facilitates matters wonderfully. Those rules of deduction laid down in that article which aroused your scorn, are invaluable to me in practical work. Observation with me is second nature. You appeared to be surprised when I told you, on our first meeting, that you had come from Afghanistan."
10 "You were told, no doubt."

"Nothing of the sort. I knew you came from Afghanistan. From long habit the train of thoughts ran so swiftly through my mind, that I arrived at the conclusion without being conscious of intermediate steps. There were such steps, however. The train
15 of reasoning ran, 'Here is a gentleman of a medical type, but with the air of a military man. Clearly an army doctor, then. He has just come from the tropics, for his face is dark, and that is not the natural tint of his skin, for his wrists are fair. He has undergone hardship and sickness, as his haggard face says
20 clearly. His left arm has been injured. He holds it in a stiff and unnatural manner. Where in the tropics could an English army doctor have seen much hardship and got his arm wounded? Clearly in Afghanistan.' The whole train of thought did not occupy a second. I then remarked that you came from
25 Afghanistan, and you were astonished."

"It is simple enough as you explain it," I said, smiling. "You remind me of Edgar Allan Poe's Dupin. I had no idea that such individuals did exist outside of stories."

Sherlock Holmes rose and lit his pipe. "No doubt you think
30 that you are complimenting me in comparing me to Dupin," he observed. "Now, in my opinion, Dupin was a very inferior fellow. That trick of his of breaking in on his friends' thoughts with an

3 **to bustle about** to move around busily – 6 **scorn** contempt *(Verachtung)* – 18 **fair** of pale skin – 19 **haggard** tired, exhausted – 27 C. Auguste **Dupin** fictional detective and police consultant created by Edgar Allan Poe in his short story "The Murders in the Rue Morgue" (1841) – 31 **inferior** of lesser quality

apropos remark after a quarter of an hour's silence is really very showy and superficial. He had some analytical genius, no doubt; but he was by no means such a phenomenon as Poe appeared to imagine."

5 "Have you read Gaboriau's works?" I asked. "Does Lecoq come up to your idea of a detective?"

Sherlock Holmes sniffed sardonically. "Lecoq was a miserable bungler," he said, in an angry voice. "He had only one thing to recommend him, and that was his energy. That book made me
10 positively ill. The question was how to identify an unknown prisoner. I could have done it in twenty-four hours. Lecoq took six months or so. It might be made a text-book for detectives to teach them what to avoid."

I felt rather indignant at having two characters whom I had
15 admired treated in this cavalier style. I walked over to the window, and stood looking out into the busy street. "This fellow may be very clever," I said to myself, "but he is certainly very conceited."

"There are no crimes and no criminals in these days," he said,
20 querulously. "What is the use of having brains in our profession. I know well that I have it in me to make my name famous. No man lives or has ever lived who has brought the same amount of study and of natural talent to the detection of crime which I have done. And what is the result? There is no crime to detect,
25 or, at most, some bungling villainy with a motive so transparent that even a Scotland Yard official can see through it."

I was still annoyed at his bumptious style of conversation. I thought it best to change the topic.

"I wonder what that fellow is looking for?" I asked, pointing
30 to a stalwart, plainly-dressed individual who was walking slowly down the other side of the street, looking anxiously at the

---

5 Émile **Gaboriau** (1832–1873) French novelist and journalist – 5 **Lecoq** fictional amateur detective created by Gaboriau in his novel "L'Affaire Lerouge" (1866) – 8 **bungler** *(sl)* incompetent person – 18 **conceited** arrogant – 20 **querulously** ['kwerʊləsli] complaining(ly) – 25 **villainy** illegal act – 27 **bumptious** arrogant, aggressive – 30 **stalwart** strong and muscular

numbers. He had a large blue envelope in his hand, and was evidently the bearer of a message.

"You mean the retired sergeant of Marines," said Sherlock Holmes.

5 "Brag and bounce!" thought I to myself. "He knows that I cannot verify his guess."

The thought had hardly passed through my mind when the man whom we were watching caught sight of the number on our door, and ran rapidly across the roadway. We heard a loud
10 knock, a deep voice below, and heavy steps ascending the stair.

"For Mr. Sherlock Holmes," he said, stepping into the room and handing my friend the letter.

Here was an opportunity of taking the conceit out of him. He
15 little thought of this when he made that random shot. "May I ask, my lad," I said, in the blandest voice, "what your trade may be?"

"Commissionaire, sir," he said, gruffly. "Uniform away for repairs."

20 "And you were?" I asked, with a slightly malicious glance at my companion.

"A sergeant, sir, Royal Marine Light Infantry, sir. No answer? Right, sir."

He clicked his heels together, raised his hand in a salute, and
25 was gone.

---

5 **Brag and bounce!** *(old)* exclamation of annoyance – 18 **Commissionaire** member of the Corps of Commissionaires, which provides employment for former members of the armed services – 18 **gruffly** brusquely – 20 **malicious** *here:* aggressive, annoyed

Story 4: A Scandal in Bohemia (1891)

by Sir Arthur Conan Doyle

*Editor's note. The illustrations here are reproductions of the
original drawings that accompanied this text in 1891. They were*
5 *drawn by Sidney Paget (1860–1908). For reasons of space and
economy, we have not reproduced all of them – an excellent review
of all illustrations to Doyle's work, including all ten that go with
"A Scandal in Bohemia", can be seen at the very good* arthur-
conan-doyle.com.

10 **Chapter I**

To Sherlock Holmes she is always *the* woman. I have seldom
heard him mention her under any other name. In his eyes she
eclipses and predominates the whole of her sex. It was not that
he felt any emotion akin to love for Irene Adler. All emotions,
15 and that one particularly, were abhorrent to his cold, precise
but admirably balanced mind. He was, I take it, the most perfect
reasoning and observing machine that the world has seen, but
as a lover he would have placed himself in a false position. He
never spoke of the softer passions, save with a gibe and a sneer.
20 They were admirable things for the observer—excellent for
drawing the veil from men's motives and actions. But for the
trained reasoner to admit such intrusions into his own delicate
and finely adjusted temperament was to introduce a distracting
factor which might throw a doubt upon all his mental results.
25 Grit in a sensitive instrument, or a crack in one of his own high-
power lenses, would not be more disturbing than a strong

---

11 **seldom** rarely – 13 **to eclipse sb** to outshine sb – 14 **akin** similar – 15 **abhorrent**
repulsive, hated – 19 **gibe** sarcastic joke – 22 **to admit an intrusion** to let sb in – 25 **grit**
fine sand or stones

emotion in a nature such as his. And yet there was but one woman to him, and that woman was the late Irene Adler, of dubious and questionable memory.

I had seen little of Holmes lately. My marriage had drifted us
5 away from each other. My own complete happiness, and the home-centred interests which rise up around the man who first finds himself master of his own establishment, were sufficient to absorb all my attention, while Holmes, who loathed every form of society with his whole Bohemian soul, remained in our
10 lodgings in Baker Street, buried among his old books, and alternating from week to week between cocaine and ambition, the drowsiness of the drug, and the fierce energy of his own keen nature. He was still, as ever, deeply attracted by the study of crime, and occupied his immense faculties and extraordinary
15 powers of observation in following out those clues, and clearing up those mysteries which had been abandoned as hopeless by the official police. From time to time I heard some vague account of his doings: of his summons to Odessa in the case of the Trepoff murder, of his clearing up of the singular tragedy of the Atkinson
20 brothers at Trincomalee, and finally of the mission which he had accomplished so delicately and successfully for the reigning family of Holland. Beyond these signs of his activity, however, which I merely shared with all the readers of the daily press, I knew little of my former friend and companion.

25 One night—it was on the twentieth of March, 1888—I was returning from a journey to a patient (for I had now returned to civil practice), when my way led me through Baker Street. As I passed the well-remembered door, which must always be associated in my mind with my wooing, and with the dark
30 incidents of the Study in Scarlet, I was seized with a keen desire to see Holmes again, and to know how he was employing his

---

3 **dubious** doubtful – 8 **to loathe** [ləʊθ] to hate very much – 9 **Bohemian** *here:* unconventional – 18 **summons** act of an official asking/ ordering sb to come to a place – 20 **Trincomalee** town on the East coast of Sri Lanka – 29 **to woo (sb)** *(old)* to go out with sb, meet sb of the opposite sex with a view to marrying them – 30 **Study in Scarlet** Holmes and Watson's first case together (see page 40 of this book)

extraordinary powers. His rooms were brilliantly lit, and, even as I looked up, I saw his tall, spare figure pass twice in a dark silhouette against the blind. He was pacing the room swiftly, eagerly, with his head sunk upon his chest and his hands clasped
5 behind him. To me, who knew his every mood and habit, his attitude and manner told their own story. He was at work again. He had risen out of his drug-created dreams and was hot upon the scent of some new problem. I rang the bell and was shown up to the chamber which had formerly been in part my own.

10 His manner was not effusive. It seldom was; but he was glad, I think, to see me. With hardly a word spoken, but with a kindly eye, he waved me to an armchair, threw across his case of cigars, and indicated a spirit case and a gasogene in the corner. Then he stood before the fire and looked me over in his singular
15 introspective fashion.

"Wedlock suits you," he remarked. "I think, Watson, that you have put on seven and a half pounds since I saw you."

"Seven!" I answered.

"Indeed, I should have thought a little more. Just a trifle more,
20 I fancy, Watson. And in practice again, I observe. You did not tell me that you intended to go into harness."

"Then, how do you know?"

"I see it, I deduce it. How do I know that you have been getting yourself very wet lately, and that you have a most clumsy and
25 careless servant girl?"

"My dear Holmes," said I, "this is too much. You would certainly have been burned, had you lived a few centuries ago. It is true that I had a country walk on Thursday and came home in a dreadful mess, but as I have changed my clothes I can't imagine
30 how you deduce it. As to Mary Jane, she is incorrigible, and my wife has given her notice, but there, again, I fail to see how you work it out."

---

10 **effusive** talkative – 13 **gasogene** an old-fashioned device for producing sparkling water – 16 **wedlock** the state of being married – 19 **a trifle** a little bit – 21 **to go into harness** (*fig*) to find a regular job – 23 **to deduce** to analyse and conclude – 31 **to give sb notice** (*fml*) to dismiss sb (from their job)

He chuckled to himself and rubbed his long, nervous hands together.

"It is simplicity itself," said he; "my eyes tell me that on the inside of your left shoe, just where the firelight strikes it, the
5 leather is scored by six almost parallel cuts. Obviously they have been caused by someone who has very carelessly scraped round the edges of the sole in order to remove crusted mud from it. Hence, you see, my double deduction that you had been out in vile weather, and that you had a particularly malignant boot-
10 slitting specimen of the London slavey. As to your practice, if a gentleman walks into my rooms smelling of iodoform, with a black mark of nitrate of silver upon his right forefinger, and a bulge on the right side of his top-hat to show where he has secreted his stethoscope, I must be dull, indeed, if I do not
15 pronounce him to be an active member of the medical profession."

I could not help laughing at the ease with which he explained his process of deduction. "When I hear you give your reasons," I remarked, "the thing always appears to me to be so ridiculously
20 simple that I could easily do it myself, though at each successive instance of your reasoning I am baffled until you explain your process. And yet I believe that my eyes are as good as yours."

"Quite so," he answered, lighting a cigarette, and throwing himself down into an armchair. "You see, but you do not observe.
25 The distinction is clear. For example, you have frequently seen the steps which lead up from the hall to this room."

"Frequently."

"How often?"

"Well, some hundreds of times."
30 "Then how many are there?"

"How many? I don't know."

---

5 **to score** *here:* to scratch marks into a surface – 8 **hence** therefore – 9 **vile** extremely unpleasant – 9 **malignant** evil – 10 **specimen** *(usu pej)* type of person – 10 **slavey** *here:* servants – 11 **iodoform** chemical used in hospitals – 13 **bulge** lump – 13 **top-hat** cylinder hat – 20 **successive** [sək'sesɪv] *aufeinanderfolgend* – 21 **baffled** amazed, surprised

"Quite so! You have not observed. And yet you have seen. That is just my point. Now, I know that there are seventeen steps, because I have both seen and observed. By the way, since you are interested in these little problems, and since you are good
5 enough to chronicle one or two of my trifling experiences, you may be interested in this." He threw over a sheet of thick, pink-tinted notepaper which had been lying open upon the table. "It came by the last post," said he. "Read it aloud."

The note was undated, and without either signature or
10 address.

"There will call upon you tonight, at a quarter to eight o'clock," it said, "a gentleman who desires to consult you upon a matter of the very deepest moment. Your recent services to one of the royal houses of Europe have shown that you are one who may
15 safely be trusted with matters which are of an importance which can hardly be exaggerated. This account of you we have from all quarters received. Be in your chamber then at that hour, and do not take it amiss if your visitor wears a mask."

"This is indeed a mystery," I remarked. "What do you imagine
20 that it means?"

"I have no data yet. It is a capital mistake to theorise before one has data. Insensibly one begins to twist facts to suit theories, instead of theories to suit facts. But the note itself. What do you deduce from it?"

25 I carefully examined the writing, and the paper upon which it was written.

"The man who wrote it was presumably well to do," I remarked, endeavouring to imitate my companion's processes. "Such paper could not be bought under half a crown a packet. It is peculiarly
30 strong and stiff."

"Peculiar—that is the very word," said Holmes. "It is not an English paper at all. Hold it up to the light."

---

11 **to call upon sb** to ask sb for help or advice – 13 **moment** importance – 17 **all quarters** everybody who was asked – 18 **to take sth amiss** to resent sb's doing sth – 21 **capital** huge – 27 **well to do** *(coll)* rich

I did so, and saw a large 'E' with a small 'g', a 'P', and a large 'G' with a small 't' woven into the texture of the paper.

"What do you make of that?" asked Holmes.

"The name of the maker, no doubt; or his monogram,
5 rather."

"Not at all. The 'G' with the small 't' stands for 'Gesellschaft,' which is the German for 'Company.' It is a customary contraction like our 'Co.' 'P,' of course, stands for 'Papier.' Now for the 'Eg.' Let us glance at our Continental Gazetteer." He took down a
10 heavy brown volume from his shelves. "Eglow, Eglonitz—here we are, Egria. It is in a German-speaking country—in Bohemia, not far from Carlsbad. 'Remarkable as being the scene of the death of Wallenstein, and for its numerous glass-factories and paper-mills.' Ha, ha, my boy, what do you make of that?" His
15 eyes sparkled, and he sent up a great blue triumphant cloud from his cigarette.

"The paper was made in Bohemia," I said.

"Precisely. And the man who wrote the note is a German. Do you note the peculiar construction of the sentence—'This
20 account of you we have from all quarters received.' A Frenchman or Russian could not have written that. It is the German who is so uncourteous to his verbs. It only remains, therefore, to discover what is wanted by this German who writes upon Bohemian paper and prefers wearing a mask to showing his face. And here
25 he comes, if I am not mistaken, to resolve all our doubts."

As he spoke there was the sharp sound of horses' hoofs and grating wheels against the curb, followed by a sharp pull at the bell. Holmes whistled.

"A pair, by the sound," said he. "Yes," he continued, glancing
30 out of the window. "A nice little brougham and a pair of beauties.

---

7 **customary** usual – 7 **contraction** *here:* abbreviation – 9 **Continental Gazetteer** geographical directory used in combination with an atlas – 13 **Wallenstein** (1583–1634) famous Bohemian military leader and politician – 22 **uncourteous** *(old)* impolite, discourteous – 27 **curb** *Bordstein* – 30 **brougham** ['bru:əm] four-wheeled carriage drawn by horses

A hundred and fifty guineas apiece. There's money in this case, Watson, if there is nothing else."

"I think that I had better go, Holmes."

"Not a bit, Doctor. Stay where you are. I am lost without my
5 Boswell. And this promises to be interesting. It would be a pity to miss it."

"But your client—"

"Never mind him. I may want your help, and so may he. Here he comes. Sit down in that armchair, Doctor, and give us your
10 best attention."

A slow and heavy step, which had been heard upon the stairs and in the passage, paused immediately outside the door.
15 Then there was a loud and authoritative tap.

"Come in!" said Holmes.

A man entered who could hardly have been less than six
20 feet six inches in height, with the chest and limbs of a Hercules. His dress was rich with a richness which would, in England, be looked upon as
25 akin to bad taste. Heavy bands of astrakhan were slashed across the sleeves and fronts of his double-breasted coat, while the deep blue cloak which was
30 thrown over his shoulders was lined with flame-coloured silk

"A MAN ENTERED."

---

1 **guinea** ['gɪni] gold coin, originally worth one (British) pound. After being replaced in 1816 by the sovereign, the term "guinea" came to mean one pound and one shilling, which is the meaning here. – 5 **James Boswell** (1740–95) friend and biographer of famous English author Samuel Johnson – 26 **astrakhan** [ˌæstrəˈkæn] fur of a Russian breed of domestic sheep

and secured at the neck with a brooch which consisted of a single flaming beryl. Boots which extended halfway up his calves, and which were trimmed at the tops with rich brown fur, completed the impression of barbaric opulence which was suggested by his whole appearance. He carried a broad-brimmed hat in his hand, while he wore across the upper part of his face, extending down past the cheekbones, a black vizard mask, which he had apparently adjusted that very moment, for his hand was still raised to it as he entered. From the lower part of the face he appeared to be a man of strong character, with a thick, hanging lip, and a long, straight chin suggestive of resolution pushed to the length of obstinacy.

"You had my note?" he asked with a deep harsh voice and a strongly marked German accent. "I told you that I would call." He looked from one to the other of us, as if uncertain which to address.

"Pray take a seat," said Holmes. "This is my friend and colleague, Dr. Watson, who is occasionally good enough to help me in my cases. Whom have I the honour to address?"

"You may address me as the Count Von Kramm, a Bohemian nobleman. I understand that this gentleman, your friend, is a man of honour and discretion, whom I may trust with a matter of the most extreme importance. If not, I should much prefer to communicate with you alone."

I rose to go, but Holmes caught me by the wrist and pushed me back into my chair. "It is both, or none," said he. "You may say before this gentleman anything which you may say to me."

The Count shrugged his broad shoulders. "Then I must begin," said he, "by binding you both to absolute secrecy for two years; at the end of that time the matter will be of no importance. At present it is not too much to say that it is of such weight it may have an influence upon European history."

---

2 **beryl** ['berᵊl] precious stone which can be transparent, green, pink or yellow –
7 **vizard** oval mask of black velvet, *usu* worn by women – 12 **obstinacy** stubbornness –
17 **pray** *(old, fml)* please

"I promise," said Holmes.

"And I."

"You will excuse this mask," continued our strange visitor. "The august person who employs me wishes his agent to be unknown to you, and I may confess at once that the title by which I have just called myself is not exactly my own."

"I was aware of it," said Holmes dryly.

"The circumstances are of great delicacy, and every precaution has to be taken to quench what might grow to be an immense scandal and seriously compromise one of the reigning families of Europe. To speak plainly, the matter implicates the great House of Ormstein, hereditary kings of Bohemia."

"I was also aware of that," murmured Holmes, settling himself down in his armchair and closing his eyes.

Our visitor glanced with some apparent surprise at the languid, lounging figure of the man who had been no doubt depicted to him as the most incisive reasoner and most energetic agent in Europe. Holmes slowly reopened his eyes and looked impatiently at his gigantic client.

"If your Majesty would condescend to state your case," he remarked, "I should be better able to advise you."

The man sprang from his chair and paced up and down the room in uncontrollable agitation. Then, with a gesture of desperation, he tore the mask from his face and hurled it upon the ground. "You are right," he cried, "I am the King. Why should I attempt to conceal it?"

"Why, indeed?" murmured Holmes. "Your Majesty had not spoken before I was aware that I was addressing Wilhelm Gottsreich Sigismond von Ormstein, Grand Duke of Cassel-Felstein, and hereditary King of Bohemia."

---

4 **august** [ɔːˈgʌst] dignified, noble – 9 **to quench** to calm, to quiet – 10 **to compromise** to harm sb's reputation – 12 **hereditary** [hɪˈredɪtᵊri] ancestral, inherited – 15 **languid** unenthusiastic – 16 **to lounge** to sit, stand or lie around comfortably – 17 **incisive** exact, ruthless – 17 **reasoner** sb who uses his intelligence and powers of deduction – 20 **to condescend to do sth** (usu ironic) to reluctantly do sth that is actually too unimportant for you to do (sich herablassen, etw zu tun)

"But you can understand," said our strange visitor, sitting down once more and passing his hand over his high white forehead, "you can understand that I am not accustomed to doing such business in my own person. Yet the matter was so
5 delicate that I could not confide it to an agent without putting myself in his power. I have come incognito from Prague for the purpose of consulting you."

"Then, pray consult," said Holmes, shutting his eyes once more.

10 "The facts are briefly these: Some five years ago, during a lengthy visit to Warsaw, I made the acquaintance of the well-known adventuress, Irene Adler. The name is no doubt familiar to you."

"Kindly look her up in my index, Doctor," murmured Holmes
15 without opening his eyes. For many years he had adopted a system of docketing all paragraphs concerning men and things, so that it was difficult to name a subject or a person on which he could not at once furnish information. In this case I found her biography sandwiched in between that of a Hebrew rabbi
20 and that of a staff-commander who had written a monograph upon the deep-sea fishes.

"Let me see!" said Holmes. "Hum! Born in New Jersey in the year 1858. Contralto—hum! La Scala, hum! Prima donna Imperial Opera of Warsaw—yes! Retired from operatic stage—ha!
25 Living in London—quite so! Your Majesty, as I understand, became entangled with this young person, wrote her some compromising letters, and is now desirous of getting those letters back."

"Precisely so. But how—"
30 "Was there a secret marriage?"
"None."
"No legal papers or certificates?"

3 **to be accustomed to doing sth** to be used to doing sth – 16 **to docket** to arrange according to a certain system of classification – 20 **monograph** *(old)* text of book length – 23 **contralto** *(mus) Altsängerin* – 23 **La Scala** famous opera house in Milan, Italy – 26 **to become entangled with sb** to get romantically involved with sb

"None."

"Then I fail to follow your Majesty. If this young person should produce her letters for blackmailing or other purposes, how is she to prove their authenticity?"

5   "There is the writing."

"Pooh, pooh! Forgery."

"My private note-paper."

"Stolen."

"My own seal."

10   "Imitated."

"My photograph."

"Bought."

"We were both in the photograph."

"Oh, dear! That is very bad! Your Majesty has indeed commit-

15 ted an indiscretion."

"I was mad—insane."

"You have compromised yourself seriously."

"I was only Crown Prince then. I was young. I am but thirty now."

20   "It must be recovered."

"We have tried and failed."

"Your Majesty must pay. It must be bought."

"She will not sell."

"Stolen, then."

25   "Five attempts have been made. Twice burglars in my pay ransacked her house. Once we diverted her luggage when she travelled. Twice she has been waylaid. There has been no result."

"No sign of it?"

30   "Absolutely none."

Holmes laughed. "It is quite a pretty little problem," said he.

"But a very serious one to me," returned the King reproachfully.

---

3 **blackmailing** crime involving threats to reveal true or false information about a person to the public unless a demand is met – 6 **forgery** copy – 26 **to ransack** to search, to plunder – 27 **to waylay sb** to attack and rob sb

"Very, indeed. And what does she propose to do with the photograph?"

"To ruin me."

"But how?"

5   "I am about to be married."

"So I have heard."

"To Clotilde Lothman von Saxe-Meningen, second daughter of the King of Scandinavia. You may know the strict principles of her family. She is herself the very soul of delicacy. A shadow
10 of a doubt as to my conduct would bring the matter to an end."

"And Irene Adler?"

"Threatens to send them the photograph. And she will do it. I know that she will do it. You do not know her, but she has a
15 soul of steel. She has the face of the most beautiful of women, and the mind of the most resolute of men. Rather than I should marry another woman, there are no lengths to which she would not go—none."

"You are sure that she has not sent it yet?"

20 "I am sure."

"And why?"

"Because she has said that she would send it on the day when the betrothal was publicly proclaimed. That will be next Monday."

25 "Oh, then we have three days yet," said Holmes with a yawn. "That is very fortunate, as I have one or two matters of importance to look into just at present. Your Majesty will, of course, stay in London for the present?"

"Certainly. You will find me at the Langham under the name
30 of the Count Von Kramm."

"Then I shall drop you a line to let you know how we progress."

"Pray do so. I shall be all anxiety."

---

23 **betrothal** [bɪˈtrəʊðᵊl] *(old)* engagement (of marriage) – 29 **The Langham** one of the largest and grand hotels in London (first opened in 1865)

"Then, as to money?"

"You have carte blanche."

"Absolutely?"

"I tell you that I would give one of the provinces of my kingdom
5   to have that photograph."

"And for present expenses?"

The King took a heavy chamois leather bag from under his
cloak and laid it on the table.

"There are three hundred pounds in gold and seven hundred
10 in notes," he said.

Holmes scribbled a receipt upon a sheet of his note-book and
handed it to him.

"And Mademoiselle's address?" he asked.

"Is Briony Lodge, Serpentine Avenue, St. John's Wood."

15 Holmes took a note of it. "One other question," said he. "Was
the photograph a cabinet?"

"It was."

"Then, good-night, your Majesty, and I trust that we shall soon
have some good news for you. And good-night, Watson," he
20 added, as the wheels of the royal brougham rolled down the
street. "If you will be good enough to call to-morrow afternoon
at three o'clock I should like to chat this little matter over with
you."

Chapter II

25 At three o'clock precisely I was at Baker Street, but Holmes had
not yet returned. The landlady informed me that he had left the
house shortly after eight o'clock in the morning. I sat down
beside the fire, however, with the intention of awaiting him,
however long he might be. I was already deeply interested in
30 his inquiry, for, though it was surrounded by none of the grim
and strange features which were associated with the two crimes

---

2 **carte blanche** *(Fr)* permission to spend whatever is necessary – 16 **cabinet** *(old) here:*
photograph mounted on cardboard (1870s–1920s)

which I have already recorded, still, the nature of the case and the exalted station of his client gave it a character of its own. Indeed, apart from the nature of the investigation which my friend had on hand, there was something in his masterly grasp
5 of a situation, and his keen, incisive reasoning, which made it a pleasure to me to study his system of work, and to follow the quick, subtle methods by which he disentangled the most inextricable mysteries. So accustomed was I to his invariable success that the very possibility of his failing had ceased to enter
10 into my head.

It was close upon four before the door opened, and a drunken-looking groom, ill-kempt and side-whiskered,
15 with an inflamed face and dis-reputable clothes, walked into the room. Accustomed as I was to my friend's amazing powers in the use of disguises, I had
20 to look three times before I was certain that it was indeed he. With a nod he vanished into the bedroom, whence he emerged in five minutes
25 tweed-suited and respectable, as of old. Putting his hands into his pockets, he stretched out his legs in front of the fire and laughed heartily for some
30 minutes.

"A DRUNKEN-LOOKING GROOM."

---

2 **exalted** elevated, high-ranking – 2 **station** (old) social position – 7 **subtle** [ˈsʌtəl] astute, clever – 8 **inextricable** here: hard to solve – 13 **groom** person responsible for feeding and taking care of horses – 13 **ill-kempt** (old) ungepflegt – 14 **side-whiskered** (old) wearing (here: false) side whiskers (Koteletten) – 15 **disreputable** unrespectable, shabby – 23 **whence** [wents] (old) from where

"Well, really!" he cried, and then he choked and laughed again until he was obliged to lie back, limp and helpless, in the chair.

"What is it?"

5 "It's quite too funny. I am sure you could never guess how I employed my morning, or what I ended by doing."

"I can't imagine. I suppose that you have been watching the habits, and perhaps the house, of Miss Irene Adler."

"Quite so; but the sequel was rather unusual. I will tell you, 10 however. I left the house a little after eight o'clock this morning in the character of a groom out of work. There is a wonderful sympathy and freemasonry among horsey men. Be one of them, and you will know all that there is to know. I soon found Briony Lodge. It is a bijou villa, with a garden at the back, but built out 15 in front right up to the road, two storeys. Chubb lock to the door. Large sitting-room on the right side, well furnished, with long windows almost to the floor, and those preposterous English window fasteners which a child could open. Behind there was nothing remarkable, save that the passage window could be 20 reached from the top of the coach-house. I walked round it and examined it closely from every point of view, but without noting anything else of interest.

"I then lounged down the street and found, as I expected, that there was a mews in a lane which runs down by one wall of the 25 garden. I lent the ostlers a hand in rubbing down their horses, and received in exchange twopence, a glass of half-and-half, two fills of shag tobacco, and as much information as I could desire about Miss Adler, to say nothing of half a dozen other people in the neighbourhood in whom I was not in the least

---

6 **to employ** *here:* to spend, use – 12 **freemasonry** *Zusammengehörigkeitsgefühl* – 12 **horsey** *(coll)* devoted to horses – 14 **bijou** ['biːʒuː] *(adj, Fr)* very beautiful – 15 **Chubb lock** type of lock which prevents unauthorised access and leaves evidence when it has been interfered with – 17 **preposterous** [prɪˈpɒstərəs] ridiculous, absurd – 20 **coach-house** building for housing carriages – 24 **mews** [mjuːz] a row of stables *(usu* with houses for carriages and living quarters)* – 25 **(h)ostler** stableman, groom

interested, but whose biographies I was compelled to listen to."

"And what of Irene Adler?" I asked.

"Oh, she has turned all the men's heads down in that part.
5 She is the daintiest thing under a bonnet on this planet. So say the Serpentine-mews, to a man. She lives quietly, sings at concerts, drives out at five every day, and returns at seven sharp for dinner. Seldom goes out at other times, except when she sings. Has only one male visitor, but a good deal of him. He is
10 dark, handsome, and dashing, never calls less than once a day, and often twice. He is a Mr. Godfrey Norton, of the Inner Temple. See the advantages of a cabman as a confidant. They had driven him home a dozen times from Serpentine-mews, and knew all about him. When I had listened to all they had to tell, I began
15 to walk up and down near Briony Lodge once more, and to think over my plan of campaign.

"This Godfrey Norton was evidently an important factor in the matter. He was a lawyer. That sounded ominous. What was the relation between them, and what the object of his repeated
20 visits? Was she his client, his friend, or his mistress? If the former, she had probably transferred the photograph to his keeping. If the latter, it was less likely. On the issue of this question depended whether I should continue my work at Briony Lodge, or turn my attention to the gentleman's chambers in the Temple. It was a
25 delicate point, and it widened the field of my inquiry. I fear that I bore you with these details, but I have to let you see my little difficulties, if you are to understand the situation."

"I am following you closely," I answered.

"I was still balancing the matter in my mind when a hansom
30 cab drove up to Briony Lodge, and a gentleman sprang out. He was a remarkably handsome man, dark, aquiline, and

---

1 **compelled** forced – 5 **dainty** delicate, fragile, pretty – 5 **under a bonnet** *here:* female (**bonnet** = women's hat) – 11 **the (Inner) Temple** area of central London, near Temple Church, hosting the Inns of Court (a law school and offices of barristers in London) – 29 **hansom** ['hænsəm] **cab** small carriage drawn by one single horse – 31 **aquiline** ['ækwɪlaɪn] resembling an eagle

moustached—evidently the man of whom I had heard. He appeared to be in a great hurry, shouted to the cabman to wait, and brushed past the maid who opened the door with the air of a man who was thoroughly at home.

5   "He was in the house about half an hour, and I could catch glimpses of him in the windows of the sitting-room, pacing up and down, talking excitedly, and waving his arms. Of her I could see nothing. Presently he emerged, looking even more flurried than before. As he stepped up to the cab, he pulled a gold watch
10 from his pocket and looked at it earnestly, 'Drive like the devil,' he shouted, 'first to Gross & Hankey's in Regent Street, and then to the Church of St. Monica in the Edgeware Road. Half a guinea if you do it in twenty minutes!'

    "Away they went, and I was just wondering whether I should
15 not do well to follow them when up the lane came a neat little landau, the coachman with his coat only half-buttoned, and his tie under his ear, while all the tags of his harness were sticking out of the buckles. It hadn't pulled up before she shot out of the hall door and into it. I only caught a glimpse of her at the moment,
20 but she was a lovely woman, with a face that a man might die for.

    "'The Church of St. Monica, John,' she cried, 'and half a sovereign if you reach it in twenty minutes.'

    "This was quite too good to lose, Watson. I was just balancing
25 whether I should run for it, or whether I should perch behind her landau when a cab came through the street. The driver looked twice at such a shabby fare, but I jumped in before he could object. 'The Church of St. Monica,' said I, 'and half a sovereign if you reach it in twenty minutes.' It was twenty-five
30 minutes to twelve, and of course it was clear enough what was in the wind.

---

1 **moustached** wearing a moustache *(Schnurrbart)* – 8 **to emerge** to come out – 8 **flurried** nervous, excited – 16 **landau** four-wheeled convertible carriage drawn by horses – 23 **sovereign** *(old)* gold coin, worth one pound sterling (a lot of money then) – 25 **to perch** to sit *(here:* in secret) – 30 **to be in the wind** to be about to happen

"My cabby drove fast. I don't think I ever drove faster, but the others were there before us. The cab and the landau with their steaming horses were in front of the door when I arrived. I paid the man and hurried into the church. There was not a soul there save the two whom I had followed and a surpliced clergyman, who seemed to be expostulating with them. They were all three standing in a knot in front of the altar. I lounged up the side aisle like any other idler who has dropped into a church. Suddenly, to my surprise, the three at the altar faced round to me, and Godfrey Norton came running as hard as he could towards me.

" 'Thank God,' he cried. 'You'll do. Come! Come!'

" 'What then?' I asked.

" 'Come, man, come, only three minutes, or it won't be legal.'

"I was half-dragged up to the altar, and before I knew where I was I found myself mumbling responses which were whispered in my ear, and vouching for things of which I knew nothing, and generally assisting in the secure tying up of Irene Adler, spinster, to Godfrey Norton, bachelor. It was all done in an instant, and there was the gentleman thanking me on the one side and the lady on the other, while the clergyman beamed on me in front. It was the most preposterous position in which I ever found myself in my life, and it was the thought of it that started me laughing just now. It seems that there had been some informality about their license, that the clergyman absolutely refused to marry them without a witness of some sort, and that my lucky appearance saved the bridegroom from having to sally out into the streets in search of a best man. The bride gave me a sovereign, and I mean to wear it on my watch chain in memory of the occasion."

5 **surpliced** wearing a surplice (white linen tunic worn by clergymen) – 6 **to expostulate with sb** to argue vehemently with sb – 19 **spinster** unmarried woman – 28 **to sally out** *(old, sl)* to go out

"This is a very unexpected turn of affairs," said I, "and what then?"

"Well, I found my plans very seriously menaced. It looked as if the pair might take an immediate departure, and so necessitate
5 very prompt and energetic measures on my part. At the church door, however, they separated, he driving back to the Temple, and she to her own house. 'I shall drive out in the park at five as usual,' she said as she left him. I heard no more. They drove away in different directions, and I went off to make my own
10 arrangements."

"Which are?"

"Some cold beef and a glass of beer," he answered, ringing the bell. "I have been too busy to think of food, and I am likely to be busier still this evening. By the way, Doctor, I shall want
15 your co-operation."

"I shall be delighted."

"You don't mind breaking the law?"

"Not in the least."

"Nor running a chance of arrest?"

20 "Not in a good cause."

"Oh, the cause is excellent!"

"Then I am your man."

"I was sure that I might rely on you."

"But what is it you wish?"

25 "When Mrs. Turner has brought in the tray I will make it clear to you. Now," he said as he turned hungrily on the simple fare that our landlady had provided, "I must discuss it while I eat, for I have not much time. It is nearly five now. In two hours we must be on the scene of action. Miss Irene, or Madame, rather,
30 returns from her drive at seven. We must be at Briony Lodge to meet her."

"And what then?"

3 **menaced** threatened – 26 **fare** food and drink

"You must leave that to me. I have already arranged what is to occur. There is only one point on which I must insist. You must not interfere, come what may. You understand?"

"I am to be neutral?"

5 "To do nothing whatever. There will probably be some small unpleasantness. Do not join in it. It will end in my being conveyed into the house. Four or five minutes afterwards the sitting-room window will open. You are to station yourself close to that open window."

10 "Yes."

"You are to watch me, for I will be visible to you."

"Yes."

"And when I raise my hand—so—you will throw into the room what I give you to throw, and will, at the same time, raise the
15 cry of fire. You quite follow me?"

"Entirely."

"It is nothing very formidable," he said, taking a long cigar-shaped roll from his pocket. "It is an ordinary plumber's smoke-rocket, fitted with a cap at either end to make it self-lighting.
20 Your task is confined to that. When you raise your cry of fire, it will be taken up by quite a number of people. You may then walk to the end of the street, and I will rejoin you in ten minutes. I hope that I have made myself clear?"

"I am to remain neutral, to get near the window, to watch you,
25 and at the signal to throw in this object, then to raise the cry of fire, and to wait you at the corner of the street."

"Precisely."

"Then you may entirely rely on me."

"That is excellent. I think, perhaps, it is almost time that I
30 prepare for the new role I have to play."

---

2 to occur to take place – **7 to be conveyed** *here:* to be carried – 18 **plumber's smoke-rocket** smoke bomb used by plumbers to detect leaks in pipes

He disappeared into his bedroom and returned in a few minutes in the character of an amiable and simple-minded
5 Nonconformist clergyman. His broad black hat, his baggy trousers, his white tie, his sympathetic smile, and general look of peering and benevolent
10 curiosity were such as Mr. John Hare alone could have equalled. It was not merely that Holmes changed his costume. His expression, his manner, his
15 very soul seemed to vary with every fresh part that he assumed. The stage lost a fine actor, even as science lost an acute reasoner, when he became a specialist in crime.

"A SIMPLE MINDED CLERGYMAN."

20 It was a quarter past six when we left Baker Street, and it still wanted ten minutes to the hour when we found ourselves in Serpentine Avenue. It was already dusk, and the lamps were just being lighted as we paced up and down in front of Briony Lodge, waiting for the coming of its occupant. The house was just such
25 as I had pictured it from Sherlock Holmes' succinct description, but the locality appeared to be less private than I expected. On the contrary, for a small street in a quiet neighbourhood, it was remarkably animated. There was a group of shabbily dressed men smoking and laughing in a corner, a scissors-grinder with
30 his wheel, two guardsmen who were flirting with a nurse-girl,

5 **Nonconformist** *(hist)* Protestant Christian who did not conform to the traditions of the established Church of England after the Act of Uniformity in 1662 – 9 **benevolent** [bɪˈnevªlənt] warm-hearted – 10 **Sir John Hare** (1844–1921) English actor and theatre manager – 25 **succinct** short and precise – 29 **scissors-grinder** person who resharpens scissors and other cutting tools

and several well-dressed young men who were lounging up and down with cigars in their mouths.

"You see," remarked Holmes, as we paced to and fro in front of the house, "this marriage rather simplifies matters. The
5 photograph becomes a double-edged weapon now. The chances are that she would be as averse to its being seen by Mr. Godfrey Norton, as our client is to its coming to the eyes of his princess. Now the question is, where are we to find the photograph?"

"Where, indeed?"

10 "It is most unlikely that she carries it about with her. It is cabinet size. Too large for easy concealment about a woman's dress. She knows that the King is capable of having her waylaid and searched. Two attempts of the sort have already been made. We may take it, then, that she does not carry it about with
15 her."

"Where, then?"

"Her banker or her lawyer. There is that double possibility. But I am inclined to think neither. Women are naturally secretive, and they like to do their own secreting. Why should she hand it
20 over to anyone else? She could trust her own guardianship, but she could not tell what indirect or political influence might be brought to bear upon a business man. Besides, remember that she had resolved to use it within a few days. It must be where she can lay her hands upon it. It must be in her own house."

25 "But it has twice been burgled."

"Pshaw! They did not know how to look."

"But how will you look?"

"I will not look."

"What then?"

30 "I will get her to show me."

"But she will refuse."

"She will not be able to. But I hear the rumble of wheels. It is her carriage. Now carry out my orders to the letter."

---

6 **averse** against – 11 **for easy concealment** to be easily hidden from view – 18 **to be inclined to do sth** to tend or prefer to do sth

As he spoke the gleam of the sidelights of a carriage came round the curve of the avenue. It was a smart little landau which rattled up to the door of Briony Lodge. As it pulled up, one of the loafing men at the corner dashed forward to open the door
5 in the hope of earning a copper, but was elbowed away by another loafer, who had rushed up with the same intention. A fierce quarrel broke out, which was increased by the two guardsmen, who took sides with one of the loungers, and by the scissors-grinder, who was equally hot upon the other side. A
10 blow was struck, and in an instant the lady, who had stepped from her carriage, was the centre of a little knot of flushed and struggling men, who struck savagely at each other with their fists and sticks. Holmes dashed into the crowd to protect the lady; but, just as he reached her, he gave a cry and dropped to
15 the ground, with the blood running freely down his face. At his fall the guardsmen took to their heels in one direction and the loungers in the other, while a number of better dressed people, who had watched the scuffle without taking part in it, crowded in to help the lady and to attend to the injured man. Irene Adler,
20 as I will still call her, had hurried up the steps; but she stood at the top with her superb figure outlined against the lights of the hall, looking back into the street.

"Is the poor gentleman much hurt?" she asked.

"He is dead," cried several voices.

25 "No, no, there's life in him!" shouted another. "But he'll be gone before you can get him to hospital."

"He's a brave fellow," said a woman. "They would have had the lady's purse and watch if it hadn't been for him. They were a gang, and a rough one, too. Ah, he's breathing now."

30 "He can't lie in the street. May we bring him in, marm?"

"Surely. Bring him into the sitting-room. There is a comfortable sofa. This way, please!"

---

4 **loafing** sitting or standing around lazily, not doing anything useful – 5 **copper** coin of low value – 16 **to take one's heels** to run away – 18 **scuffle** short and harmless fight – 30 **marm** *(old)* ma'am (short for madam)

Slowly and solemnly he was borne into Briony Lodge and laid out in the principal room, while I still observed the proceedings from my post by the window. The lamps had been lit, but the blinds had not been drawn, so that I could see Holmes as he lay
5 upon the couch. I do not know whether he was seized with compunction at that moment for the part he was playing, but I know that I never felt more heartily ashamed of myself in my life than when I saw the beautiful creature against whom I was conspiring, or the grace and kindliness with which she
10 waited upon the injured man. And yet it would be the blackest treachery to Holmes to draw back now from the part which he had intrusted to me. I hardened my heart, and took the smoke-rocket from under my ulster. After all, I thought, we are not injuring her. We are but preventing her from injuring another.
15 Holmes had sat up upon the couch, and I saw him motion like a man who is in need of air. A maid rushed across and threw open the window. At the same instant I saw him raise his hand and at the signal I tossed my rocket into the room with a cry of "Fire!" The word was no sooner out of my mouth than the whole
20 crowd of spectators, well dressed and ill—gentlemen, ostlers, and servant maids—joined in a general shriek of "Fire!" Thick clouds of smoke curled through the room and out at the open window. I caught a glimpse of rushing figures, and a moment later the voice of Holmes from within assuring them that it was
25 a false alarm. Slipping through the shouting crowd I made my way to the corner of the street, and in ten minutes was rejoiced to find my friend's arm in mine, and to get away from the scene of uproar. He walked swiftly and in silence for some few minutes until we had turned down one of the quiet streets which lead
30 towards the Edgeware Road.

"You did it very nicely, Doctor," he remarked. "Nothing could have been better. It is all right."

"You have the photograph?"

---

1 **solemnly** *feierlich* – 6 **compunction** bad conscience, scruples – 13 **ulster** long, loose overcoat made of rough material – 18 **to toss** to throw – 28 **uproar** tumult

"I know where it is."

"And how did you find out?"

"She showed me, as I told you she would."

"I am still in the dark."

5   "I do not wish to make a mystery," said he, laughing. "The matter was perfectly simple. You, of course, saw that everyone in the street was an accomplice. They were all engaged for the evening."

"I guessed as much."

10   "Then, when the row broke out, I had a little moist red paint in the palm of my hand. I rushed forward, fell down, clapped my hand to my face, and became a piteous spectacle. It is an old trick."

"That also I could fathom."

15   "Then they carried me in. She was bound to have me in. What else could she do? And into her sitting-room, which was the very room which I suspected. It lay between that and her bedroom, and I was determined to see which. They laid me on a couch, I motioned for air, they were compelled to open the window, and 20 you had your chance."

"How did that help you?"

"It was all-important. When a woman thinks that her house is on fire, her instinct is at once to rush to the thing which she values most. It is a perfectly overpowering impulse, and I have 25 more than once taken advantage of it. In the case of the Darlington Substitution Scandal it was of use to me, and also in the Arnsworth Castle business. A married woman grabs at her baby; an unmarried one reaches for her jewel-box. Now it was clear to me that our lady of to-day had nothing in the house 30 more precious to her than what we are in quest of. She would rush to secure it. The alarm of fire was admirably done. The smoke and shouting were enough to shake nerves of steel. She responded beautifully. The photograph is in a recess behind a

---

10 **moist** damp, wet – 14 **to fathom** to understand – 30 **to be in quest of sth** to search for sth – 33 **recess** *Nische*

sliding panel just above the right bell-pull. She was there in an instant, and I caught a glimpse of it as she half drew it out. When I cried out that it was a false alarm, she replaced it, glanced at the rocket, rushed from the room, and I have not seen her since.
5 I rose, and, making my excuses, escaped from the house. I hesitated whether to attempt to secure the photograph at once; but the coachman had come in, and as he was watching me narrowly, it seemed safer to wait. A little over-precipitance may ruin all."

10 "And now?" I asked.

"Our quest is practically finished. I shall call with the King to-morrow, and with you, if you care to come with us. We will be shown into the sitting-room to wait for the lady, but it is probable that when she comes she may find neither us nor the
15 photograph. It might be a satisfaction to his Majesty to regain it with his own hands."

"And when will you call?"

"At eight in the morning. She will not be up, so that we shall have a clear field. Besides, we must be prompt, for this marriage
20 may mean a complete change in her life and habits. I must wire to the King without delay."

We had reached Baker Street and had stopped at the door. He was searching his pockets for the key when someone passing said:

25 "Good-night, Mister Sherlock Holmes."

There were several people on the pavement at the time, but the greeting appeared to come from a slim youth in an ulster who had hurried by.

"I've heard that voice before," said Holmes, staring down the
30 dimly lit street. "Now, I wonder who the deuce that could have been."

---

1 **bell pull** pull cord connected to a wire which rings a bell when pulled; used to summon servants – 8 **precipitance** [prɪˈsɪpɪtᵊnts] hurry, haste – 20 **to wire** to send a telegraph – 30 **deuce** [djuːs] *(old, sl)* devil

Chapter III

I slept at Baker Street that night, and we were engaged upon our toast and coffee in the morning when the King of Bohemia rushed into the room.

5   "You have really got it!" he cried, grasping Sherlock Holmes by either shoulder and looking eagerly into his face.

"Not yet."

"But you have hopes?"

"I have hopes."

10   "Then, come. I am all impatience to be gone."

"We must have a cab."

"No, my brougham is waiting."

"Then that will simplify matters." We descended and started off once more for Briony Lodge.

15   "Irene Adler is married," remarked Holmes.

"Married! When?"

"Yesterday."

"But to whom?"

"To an English lawyer named Norton."

20   "But she could not love him."

"I am in hopes that she does."

"And why in hopes?"

"Because it would spare your Majesty all fear of future annoyance. If the lady loves her husband, she does not love your

25 Majesty. If she does not love your Majesty, there is no reason why she should interfere with your Majesty's plan."

"It is true. And yet—! Well! I wish she had been of my own station! What a queen she would have made!" He relapsed into a moody silence, which was not broken until we drew up in

30 Serpentine Avenue.

The door of Briony Lodge was open, and an elderly woman stood upon the steps. She watched us with a sardonic eye as we stepped from the brougham.

32 **sardonic eye** *süffisanter Blick*

"Mr. Sherlock Holmes, I believe?" said she.

"I am Mr. Holmes," answered my companion, looking at her with a questioning and rather startled gaze.

"Indeed! My mistress told me that you were likely to call. She
5 left this morning with her husband by the 5:15 train from Charing Cross for the Continent."

"What!" Sherlock Holmes staggered back, white with chagrin and surprise. "Do you mean that she has left England?"

"Never to return."

10 "And the papers?" asked the King hoarsely. "All is lost."

"We shall see." He pushed past the servant and rushed into the drawing-room, followed by the King and myself. The furniture was scattered about in every direction, with dismantled shelves and open drawers, as if the lady had hurriedly ransacked them
15 before her flight. Holmes rushed at the bell-pull, tore back a small sliding shutter, and, plunging in his hand, pulled out a photograph and a letter. The photograph was of Irene Adler herself in evening dress, the letter was superscribed to "Sherlock Holmes, Esq. To be left till called for." My friend tore it open,
20 and we all three read it together. It was dated at midnight of the preceding night and ran in this way:

MY DEAR MR. SHERLOCK HOLMES,
You really did it very well. You took me in completely. Until after the alarm of fire, I had not a suspicion. But then, when I found
25 *how I had betrayed myself, I began to think. I had been warned against you months ago. I had been told that, if the King employed an agent, it would certainly be you. And your address had been given me. Yet, with all this, you made me reveal what you wanted to know. Even after I became suspicious, I found it hard to think*
30 *evil of such a dear, kind old clergyman. But, you know, I have been trained as an actress myself. Male costume is nothing new*

---

5 **Charing Cross** railway station in Central London – 7 **chagrin** [ˈʃægrɪn]
disappointment – 13 **dismantled** taken apart – 19 **Esq.** *(abb)* Esquire, title of respect
accorded to men in a formal situation

to me. I often take advantage of the freedom which it gives. I sent
John, the coachman, to watch you, ran upstairs, got into my
walking clothes, as I call them, and came down just as you
departed.
5   *Well, I followed you to your door, and so made sure that I was*
really an object of interest to the celebrated Mr. Sherlock Holmes.
Then I, rather imprudently, wished you good-night, and started
for the Temple to see my husband.
We both thought the best resource was flight, when pursued by
10   *so formidable an antagonist; so you will find the nest empty when*
you call to-morrow. As to the photograph, your client may rest in
peace. I love and am loved by a better man than he. The King
may do what he will without hindrance from one whom he has
cruelly wronged. I keep it only to safeguard myself, and to preserve
15   *a weapon which will always secure me from any steps which he*
might take in the future. I leave a photograph which he might
care to possess; and I remain, dear Mr. Sherlock Holmes,
Very truly yours,
IRENE NORTON, née ADLER.

20   "What a woman—oh, what a woman!" cried the King of Bohemia,
when we had all three read this epistle. "Did I not tell you how
quick and resolute she was? Would she not have made an
admirable queen? Is it not a pity that she was not on my
level?"
25   "From what I have seen of the lady, she seems, indeed, to be
on a very different level to your Majesty," said Holmes coldly. "I
am sorry that I have not been able to bring your Majesty's
business to a more successful conclusion."
    "On the contrary, my dear sir," cried the King; "nothing could
30   be more successful. I know that her word is inviolate. The
photograph is now as safe as if it were in the fire."
    "I am glad to hear your Majesty say so."

21 **epistle** letter – 30 **inviolate** unable to be broken

"I am immensely indebted to you. Pray tell me in what way I can reward you. This ring—" He slipped an emerald snake ring from his finger and held it out upon the palm of his hand.

"Your Majesty has something which I should value even more 5 highly," said Holmes.

"You have but to name it."

"This photograph!"

The King stared at him in amazement.

"THIS PHOTOGRAPH!"

10 "Irene's photograph!" he cried. "Certainly, if you wish it."

"I thank your Majesty. Then there is no more to be done 15 in the matter. I have the honour to wish you a very good morning." He bowed, and, turning away without observing the hand which the 20 King had stretched out to him, he set off in my company for his chambers.

And that was how a great scandal threatened to affect the kingdom of Bohemia, and how the best plans of Mr. Sherlock Holmes were beaten by a woman's wit. He used to make merry 25 over the cleverness of women, but I have not heard him do it of late. And when he speaks of Irene Adler, or when he refers to her photograph, it is always under the honourable title of *the woman.*

---

2 **emerald** precious green gemstone *(Smaragd)* – 24 **wit** cleverness – 24 **to make merry** to make fun of

P. D. James (1920–2014)

*"All fiction is an attempt to
create order out of disorder and
to make sense of personal
experience.*

*But the classical detective
story does this within its
own established conventions;
a central mystery which is
usually but not necessarily a
murder, a closed circle of
suspects, a detective … who
comes in like an avenging deity
to solve the crime, and a final
solution which the reader
should be able to arrive at
himself by logical deduction
from the clues.*

*This … formula … is capable of accommodating a remarkable
variety of books and talents. Within the formal constraints of the
detective novel I try to say something true about men and women
under the stress of the ultimate crime and about the society in
which they live."*

Phyllis Dorothy James was an English author of crime fiction,
best known for her fictional character, Adam Dalgliesh, who was
a New Scotland Yard police commander and poet, who
investigated in fourteen mystery novels that appeared between
1962 and 2008. Several of these crime stories were adapted for
television and broadcast worldwide.

As well as being one of Britain's foremost authors of crime
fiction, James had a full-time career in the civil service, which,
she always claimed, provided her with material for her books.
She worked in the National Health Service from 1949, then at
the Home Office from 1968 for the police, in the forensic science

service. Possibly as a result of this, many of her novels have an air of officialdom and are often set in government offices. She retired from public service in 1979.

In 1983, she received an OBE and in 1991 she was made a life
5 peer, which entitled her to a seat in the House of Lords.

The following story was one of her last. It was published in 2010 and shortlisted by the Crime Writers' Association. It is not a typical detective story; more an example of a man "under the stress of the ultimate crime".

10 *[Editor's note: The last executions in the United Kingdom were by hanging, and took place in 1964. Capital punishment for murder was abolished in 1965 in Great Britain (1973 in Northern Ireland). Although unused, the death penalty remained a legal punishment for certain crimes (e.g. treason) until it was completely*
15 *abolished in 1998.]*

14 **treason** *Landesverrat*

Story 5: The Part-Time Job (2010)

by P. D. James

By the time you read this I shall be dead. Dead for how long, of
course, I cannot predict. I shall place this document in the
5 strongroom of my bank with instructions that it shall be sent to
the daily newspaper with the largest circulation on the first
working day after my funeral. My only regret is that I shan't be
alive to savour my retrospective triumph. But that is of small
account. I savour it every day of my life. I shall have done the
10 one thing I resolved to do when I was twelve years old – and the
world will know it. And the world will be interested, make no
mistake about that! I can tell you the precise date when I made
up my mind that I would kill Keith Manston-Green. We were
both pupils at St Chad's School on the Surrey borders, he the
15 only child of a wealthy businessman with a chain of garages, I
from a more humble background, who would never have arrived
at St Chad's except for the help of a scholarship endowed by a
former pupil and named after him. My six years from eleven to
seventeen were years of hell. Keith Manston-Green was the
20 school bully and I was his natural, almost inevitable victim: a
scholarship boy, timid, undersized, bespectacled, who never
spoke of his parents, was never visited at half-term, wore a
uniform that was obviously second-hand and was, like the runt
of the litter, destined to be trampled on.
25 For six years during term-time I woke every morning in fear.
The masters – some of them at least – must have known what
was happening, but it seemed to me they were part of the
conspiracy. And Manston-Green was clever. There were never
any obvious bruises: the torment was subtler than that.

8 **to savour** to make the most of sth – 8 **retrospective** looking back – 16 **humble**
modest, simple – 17 **endowed** granted, given – 21 **bespectacled** wearing glasses –
23 **runt (of the litter)** the youngest and weakest animal of a litter (= *Wurf*) – 29 **subtle**
['sʌtəl] *here:* secretive

He was clever in other ways too. Sometimes he would admit me temporarily into his circle of sycophants, give me sweets, share his tuck, stick up for me against the other boys, giving hope to me that all this signalled a change. But there never was a change. There's no point in my reciting the details of his ingenuities. It is enough to say that at six o'clock in the evening on the fifteenth of February 1932, when I was twelve years old, I made a solemn vow: one day I would kill Keith Manston-Green. That vow kept me going for the next five years of torment and remained with me, as strong as when it was first made, through all the years that followed. It may seem odd to you, reading this after my death, that killing Manston-Green should be a lifelong obsession. Surely even childhood cruelty is forgotten at last, or at least put out of mind. But not that cruelty; not my mind. In destroying my childhood, Manston-Green had made me what I am. I knew too that if I forgot that childish oath I would die bitter with regret and self-humiliation. I was in no hurry, but it was something I had to do.

My father had inherited the family business on the fringes of London's East End. He was a locksmith and taught me the trade. The shop was bombed in the war, killing both my parents, but government money compensated for the loss. The house and the shop were rebuilt and I started again. The shop wasn't the only thing I inherited from that secretive, obsessive and unhappy man. I had, like my father had, a part-time job.

Through all the years, I kept track of Keith Manston-Green. I could, of course, have received regular news of him by placing my name on the distribution list for the annual magazine of St Chad's Old Boys Society, but that seemed to me unwise. I wanted St Chad's to forget I had ever existed. I would rely on my own researches. It wasn't difficult. Manston-Green, like me, had inherited the family business and, motoring through Surrey, I

---

2 **sycophant** *(fml)* person who lowers him/herself to another, flatterer *(Schmeichler)* –
3 **tuck** *(old)* sweets – 6 **ingenuity** [ˌɪndʒɪˈnjuːəti] inventiveness – 19 **fringe** edge, outskirts

would note every garage I passed which bore his name. I had no difficulty, either, in finding out where he lived. Waiting for my Morris Minor to be filled, I would occasionally say, "There seems to be quite a number of Manston-Green garages in this
5 part of the world. Is it a private company or something?"

Sometimes the answer would be, "Search me, guv, haven't a clue." But other times I got a nugget of information to add to my store. "Yeah, it's still owned by the family. Keith Manston-Green. Lives outside Stonebridge." After that it was only a
10 question of consulting the local telephone directory and finding the house.

It was the kind of house I would have expected. A new red-brick monstrosity with gables and mock-Tudor beams, a large garage attached which could take up to four cars, a wide drive
15 and a high privet hedge for privacy, all enclosed in a red-brick wall. A board on the wall said, in mock-antique script, Manston Lodge.

I wasn't in any particular hurry to kill him. What was important was to make sure that the deed was done without suspicion
20 settling on me and, if possible, that the first attempt was successful. It was one of my constant pleasures, scheming over possible methods. But I knew that this mental anticipation could be dangerously self-indulgent. There would come a moment when planning, however satisfying, must give way to action.

25 When the war broke out in 1939 my fear, greater than that of the bombing, was that Manston-Green would be killed. The thought that he would die in action and be remembered as a hero was intolerable, but I need not have worried. He joined the RAF, but not as a flier. Those coveted wings were never stitched
30 above the breast pocket of his uniform. He was a Wingless

3 **Morris Minor** British car manufactured between 1948 and 1972 – 13 **gable** (of a house) *Giebel* – 13 **mock-Tudor** (of architecture) resembling the Medieval architecture of the Tudor period (1485–1603), but in fact fake – 15 **privet** *Liguster* – 23 **self-indulgent** *genießerisch* – 29 **RAF** *(abb)* Royal Air Force – 29 **coveted** desirable, much in demand – 30 **Wingless Wonder** *(sl, off)* RAF ground staff officer not trained as a pilot

Wonder, as I believe the RAF called them. I think he had something to do with equipment or maintenance and he must have been effective. He ended as a Wing Commander, and naturally he kept the rank in civilian life. His sycophants called
5 him the Wingco – and how he revelled in it.

It was in 1953 that I decided to begin taking active steps towards his elimination. The shop was modestly successful and I had a manager and an assistant, both reliable. My part-time job was an excuse for short absences and I could confidently
10 leave them in charge. I began making short visits to Stonebridge, a prosperous town on the fringes of the commuter belt where my enemy lived. Perhaps the words "held court" would be more appropriate. He was a member of the local council and of one or two charitable trusts, the kind that confer prestige rather than
15 making unwelcome financial demands, and he was captain of the golf club. Oh yes indeed, he was the "Wingco", strutting about the clubhouse as he must once have strutted in the Mess.

By then I had discovered quite a lot about Keith Manston-Green. He had divorced his wife, who had left him, taking their
20 two children, and he was now married to Shirley May, twelve years his junior. But it was his captaincy of the Stonebridge Golf Club that gave me an idea how I could get close to him.

I could tell within five minutes of entering the clubhouse that the place reeked of petty suburban snobbery. They didn't actually
25 say what prospective members would be welcome, but I could tell that there was a set of clearly understood conventions designed to enable the members to feel superior to all but the chosen few, most of them successful local businessmen. However, they were as keen on increasing their income as were
30 less snobbish enterprises and it was possible to pay green fees and enjoy a round, either alone or with a partner if one could

---

5 **to revel in sth** to enjoy sth very much – 11 **commuter belt** outskirts surrounding a metropolitan area from which it is still practical to commute (= *pendeln)* to work – 14 **to confer** to grant, to give – 16 **to strut about** to walk around confidently – 24 **to reek** *(fig)* to smell bad *(riechen)* – 24 **petty** insignificant, trivial

find one, and to take lessons from the pro. I gave a false name, of course, and paid always in cash. I was exactly the kind of interloper that no one took much notice of. Certainly no one evinced any desire to partner me. I would drink a solitary beer,
5 have my lesson and quietly depart. The undersized, ordinary-looking, bespectacled boy had grown into an undersized, ordinary-looking, bespectacled man. I had grown a moustache but there was otherwise little change. I had no fear that Manston-Green would recognise me but, taking no risks, I kept well out
10 of his way.

And did I recognise Manston-Green when I first saw him after so many years? How could I fail to do so? He too was a grown-up version of the tormentor of my childhood. He was still tall but stout, carrying his stomach high, red-faced, loud-voiced, the
15 black hair sleeked back. I could see that he was deferred to. He was the Wingco, Keith Manston-Green, prosperous businessman, provider of jobs and silver cups, slapper of backs, dispenser of free drinks.

And then I saw Shirley May, his second wife, drinking with
20 her cronies at the bar. Shirley May. She was always called by that double first name, and behind her husband's back I occasionally caught their salacious whispers, "Shirley May, but on the other hand, she may not!" He had got his trophy wife, blonde, though obviously not naturally so, voluptuous, long-legged, a second-
25 hand film-star vision of feminine desirability. Even to look at her, standing at the club bar flirting with a group of bemused fools, made me sick.

It was then that I first began to see how I might kill her husband. And not only kill him, but make him suffer over months of
30 protracted agony, just as he had made me suffer for years. The revenge wouldn't be perfect, but it would be as close as I could get.

---

3 **interloper** intruder – 4 **to evince** to show – 20 **crony** *(sl)* sychophantic friend –
22 **salacious** [sə'leɪʃəs] suggestive – 24 **voluptuous** [və'lʌptʃuəs] (of a body) well-shaped – 30 **protracted** lengthy

The months I spent leading up to action had to be carefully planned. It was important that Manston-Green did not see me, or at least not close enough to recognise me, and that he never heard even my false name. That wasn't difficult. He played only
5 at weekends and in the evenings, I chose Wednesday mornings. Even when our visits had coincided, the Wingco was far too important to cast his eyes on undistinguished temporary players only permitted on the greens because their fees were needed. It was important, too, that I didn't become even remotely
10 interesting to other members. It was necessary to play badly, and on the few occasions that someone condescended to partner me, I played badly. That took some skill: I naturally have a very good eye. I had my story ready. I had an elderly and ailing mother living in the neighbourhood and was paying occasional dutiful
15 visits. I embarked on boring descriptions of her symptoms and prognosis and would watch their eyes glazing over as they edged away. I kept my appearances infrequent; I did not want to become an object of gossip and curiosity even if both were dismissive. I needed to be too anonymous even to be regarded as the club
20 bore.

Firstly, I needed a key to the clubhouse. For a locksmith that wasn't difficult. By careful watching I discovered that three people had keys, Manston-Green, the club secretary, Bill Caraway, and the pro, Alistair McFee. McFee's was the easiest to get my hands
25 on. He kept it in the pocket of his jacket, which he invariably hung on the door of his office. I bided my time until, one Wednesday morning when he was occupied on the first green with a particularly demanding pupil, with gloved hands I took the key from his pocket and, locking myself in the lavatory, took
30 an impression. On my next visit, surreptitiously, I tested the key. It worked.

I then began the second part of my campaign. Late at night alone in my London office and wearing gloves, I cut out words

---

13 **ailing** ill, sickly – 16 **to glaze over** (of eyes) to express disinterest and indifference –
29 **lavatory** toilet – 30 **surreptitiously** [ˌsʌrəpˈtɪʃəsli] secretly

from the national newspapers and pasted them on to a sheet of writing paper, the kind sold in every stationer's shop. The messages, which I sent twice weekly, had small variations of wording but always the same insinuating poison. Why did you
5 marry that bitch? Don't you know she's having it off with someone else? Are you blind or something? Don't you know what Shirley May's up to? I don't like to see a decent man cheated. You should keep an eye on your wife.

Oh, they had their effect. On subsequent visits to the golf club
10 when, carefully distanced, I watched them together I knew that my carefully calculated strategy was working. There were public quarrels. Members of the club began to edge away when they were together. The Wingco was rattled – and so, of course, was she. I gave that marriage no more than two months. Which
15 meant that I couldn't delay.

I fixed the actual date two weeks ahead. Only one other thing was necessary. I made sure that the new clubs I purchased were the same make as his, a necessary extravagance. I substituted my driver for his driver, handling it always with gloves. It was
20 his prints I wanted, not mine. I made sure my final messages were received on the morning of the crucial day, his by post, hers pushed under the door when, watching, I saw him drive away for work. Hers said, If you want to know who's sending these notes, meet me in the clubhouse at nine tonight. Burn
25 this note. A friend. His said the same, but gave a time ten minutes later.

I realised, of course, that neither might come. That was a risk I took. But if they didn't, I would be in no danger. It would simply mean that I needed to find another way of killing Manston-Green.
30 I hoped it wouldn't be necessary. My plan was so perfect, the horror I had planned for him so wonderfully satisfying.

I won't distress you with details; they are not necessary. I had my keys to the clubhouse and I was waiting for her, her husband's

---

4 **to insinuate sth** to imply sth negative – 5 **to have it off with sb** *(sl)* to have a sexual relationship with sb – 13 **to rattle sb** *(inf)* to make sb nervous – 19 **driver** the longest and heaviest type of wooden golf club

driver in hand. As I said, I have a good eye. It took only two swings to kill her, three more to batter her face into a pulp. I dropped the driver, let myself out and locked the door. There was a public phone box at the end of the lane. When I asked for
5 the police I was put through promptly and without trouble. I disguised my voice although it wasn't strictly necessary. It became the confused, high-pitched, terrified voice of an older man.

"I've just passed the golf club. There's screaming in the clubhouse. A woman. I think someone's killing her."
10 "And your name and address, sir?"

"No, no. I'm not getting mixed up in this. It's nothing to do with me. I just thought I ought to let you know." And with gloved hands I rang off.

They came, of course. They came just in time to see Manston-
15 Green bending over his wife's body. I couldn't have planned that. I imagined they might have been late but would still have had the club with her blood and matted hair, the fingerprints, the evidence of quarrels. But they weren't late; they were just in time.
20 I resisted the temptation to go to the trial. It was irritating to have to forgo that pleasure, but I thought it prudent. Press photographs were being taken of the crowd, and although the chance of being recognised was infinitesimally small, why risk it? And I thought it sensible to continue going occasionally to
25 the golf club, but less frequently. The talk was all of the murder, but no one bothered to include me. I took my solitary lessons and departed. He appealed, of course, and that was an anxious day for me. But the appeal failed and I knew that the end was now certain.
30 There were only three weeks between sentence and execution and they were probably the happiest of my life, not in the sense of an exultant joy, but of knowing myself at peace for the first time since I'd started at St Chad's. The week before the execution

---

2 **to batter** *(inf)* to hit repeatedly and hard – 2 **pulp** mash – 21 **to forgo** to do without sth – 21 **prudent** cautious – 23 **infinitesimal** [ˌɪnfɪnɪˈtesɪməl] very small

I was with him in spirit through every minute of every hour in that condemned cell. I knew what would happen on the morning when he would be launched out of this world and out of my mind. I pictured the arrival of the executioner the day before to
5 fulfil Home Office requirements: the dropping of a sandbag in the presence of the governor to make sure that there would be no mishap and that the length of the drop was correct. I was with him as he peered through the spyhole in the door of the condemned cell, a cell only feet away from the execution
10 chamber. It's a merciful death if not mishandled and I knew Manston-Green would die with less pain than probably would I. The suffering was in the preceding weeks and no one could truly experience that horror but he. In imagination I lived his last night, the restless turning and twisting, the strengthening
15 light of the dreaded day, the breakfast he wouldn't be able to eat, the clumsy kindness of the constantly watching guards. I was with the hangman in imagination when he pinned Manston-Green's arms. I was part of that little procession which passed through the dreaded door, the white-faced governor of the prison
20 present, the chaplain keeping his eyes on his prayer book held in shaking hands.

It's a quick death, only some twenty seconds from the moment the arms are pinioned to the drop itself. But there would be one moment when he would be able to see the scaffold, the noose
25 hanging precisely at the level of his chest before the white hood was pulled into place. I exulted at the thought of those few seconds.

As usual I went to the prison the day before the execution. There were things to be done, instructions to be followed. I was
30 greeted politely but I wasn't welcome.

I knew they felt contaminated when they shook my hand. And every prisoner in every cell knew that I was there. Already there

---

7 **mishap** event that goes wrong; accident – 20 **chaplain** minister, priest – 23 **pinioned** ['pɪnjənd] tied up – 24 **scaffold** (for executions) gallows (= *Galgen*)

was the expected din, shouting voices, utensils banged against the cell doors. A little crowd of protesters or morbid voyeurs was already collecting outside the prison gate. I am a meticulous craftsman, as was my father before me. I am highly experienced
5 in my part-time job. And I think he knew me. Oh yes, he knew me. I saw the recognition in his eyes that second before I slipped the white hood over his head and pulled the lever. He dropped like a stone and the rope tautened and quivered. My life's task was at last accomplished and from now on I would be at peace.
10 I had killed Keith Manston-Green.

---

1 **din** loud and chaotic noise(s) – 3 **meticulous** precise, careful – 7 **lever** [liːˈvəʳ] *Hebel* – 8 **to tauten** (of a rope) to tighten

III. Additional material: Rules for writing detective fiction

During the so called "Golden Age" of detective fiction in the 1920s and 30s, a number of crime authors felt it necessary to introduce some ground rules for the writing of crime fiction, thus submitting themselves to different catalogues of "Do's and
5 Don'ts".

Among these writers was the American art critic **Willard Huntington Wright** (1888–1939), who is best known today for creating the famous fictional detective Philo Vance under the pseudonym **S. S. Van Dine**. His protagonist was very popular
10 and, having successfully solved crimes in a book series, he became a hero known to an even wider public in radio drama series and several films.

While recovering from a serious cocaine addiction, Van Dine had begun reading detective novels out of boredom and,
15 intrigued, had started to research the genre as well as write detective fiction himself. His introduction to the anthology *The World's Great Detective Stories* (1928) is still widely known today, as is the following set of rules for writing detective stories, which was published in the same year as an article for *The American*
20 *Magazine* and became an important document for the critical study of detective fiction.

We have rounded off this section, and the book, with two further (briefer) sets of "crime fiction commandments", one based on the ideas of Englishman **Ronald Knox** (1888–1957)
25 and the last one on rules formulated by perhaps the most famous crime fiction author of the 20th Century of them all, US American, **Raymond Chandler** (1888–1959).

1. Twenty Rules for Writing Detective Stories (1928)

by S. S. Van Dine

1. The reader must have equal opportunity with the detective
for solving the mystery. All clues must be plainly stated and
described.

2. No wilful tricks or deceptions may be played on the reader
other than those played legitimately by the criminal on the
detective himself.

3. There must be no love interest in the story. To introduce amour
is to clutter up a purely intellectual experience with irrelevant
sentiment. The business in hand is to bring a criminal to the
bar of justice, not to bring a lovelorn couple to the hymeneal
altar.

4. The detective himself, or one of the official investigators,
should never turn out to be the culprit. This is bald trickery,
on a par with offering someone a bright penny for a five-dollar
gold piece. It's false pretenses.

5. The culprit must be determined by logical deductions – not
by accident or coincidence or unmotivated confession. To solve
a criminal problem in this latter fashion is like sending the reader
on a deliberate wild-goose chase, and then telling him, after he
has failed, that you had the object of his search up your sleeve
all the time. Such an author is no better than a practical joker.

---

11 **to clutter up** to mix up, to get sth in a mess – 12 **sentiment** emotion – 13 **lovelorn** *liebeskrank* – 13 **hymeneal altar** [haɪˌmeniːəl.ˈɔːltəʳ] marriage altar – 16 **culprit** guilty person *(Täter)* – 16 **bald** blunt – 17 **to be on a par with sth** to be the same as sth – 23 **to have/hide sth up your sleeve** to hide sth so that you can reveal it later (like a magician)

6. The detective novel must have a detective in it; and a detective is not a detective unless he detects. His function is to gather clues that will eventually lead to the person who did the dirty work in the first chapter; and if the detective does not reach his conclusions through an analysis of those clues, he has no more solved his problem than the schoolboy who gets his answer out of the back of the arithmetic.

7. There simply must be a corpse in a detective novel, and the deader the corpse the better. No lesser crime than murder will suffice. Three hundred pages is far too much bother for a crime other than murder. After all, the reader's trouble and expenditure of energy must be rewarded. Americans are essentially humane, and therefore a tiptop murder arouses their sense of vengeance and horror. They wish to bring the perpetrator to justice; and when "murder most foul, as in the best it is," has been committed, the chase is on with all the righteous enthusiasm of which the thrice gentle reader is capable.

8. The problem of the crime must be solved by strictly naturalistic means. Such methods for learning the truth as slate-writing, ouija-boards, mind-reading, spiritualistic séances, crystal-gazing, and the like, are taboo. A reader has a chance when matching his wits with a rationalistic detective, but if he must compete with the world of spirits and go chasing about the fourth dimension of metaphysics, he is defeated ab initio.

9. There must be but one detective – that is, but one protagonist of deduction – one deus ex machina. To bring the minds of three or four, or sometimes a gang of detectives to bear on a problem

---

7 **arithmetic** *(old) here:* book – 10 **to suffice** to be enough – 10 **bother** trouble – 11 **expenditure** using up (of energy and resources) – 16 **righteous** ['raɪtʃəs] true, justifiable – 19 **slate-writing** alleged psychic ability allowing a person to produce written words without consciously writing – 20 **ouija-board** ['wiːdʒə] flat board marked with letters and numbers used during seances to communicate with spirits – 24 **ab initio** *(Lat)* from the start – 26 **deus ex machina** *(Lat) here:* person responsible for solving the crime

is not only to disperse the interest and break the direct thread of logic, but to take an unfair advantage of the reader, who, at the outset, pits his mind against that of the detective and proceeds to do mental battle. If there is more than one detective,
5 the reader doesn't know who his co-deductor is. It's like making the reader run a race with a relay team.

10. The culprit must turn out to be a person who has played a more or less prominent part in the story – that is, a person with whom the reader is familiar and in whom he takes an interest.
10 For a writer to fasten the crime, in the final chapter, on a stranger or person who has played a wholly unimportant part in the tale, is to confess to his inability to match wits with the reader.

11. Servants – butlers, footmen, valets, game-keepers, cooks – must not be chosen by the author as the culprit. This is begging
15 a noble question. It is a too easy solution. It is unsatisfactory, and makes the reader feel that his time has been wasted. The culprit must be a decidedly worth-while person – one that wouldn't ordinarily come under suspicion; for if the crime was the sordid work of a menial, the author would have had no
20 business to embalm it in book-form.

12. There must be but one culprit, no matter how many murders are committed. The culprit may, of course, have a minor helper or co-plotter; but the entire onus must rest on one pair of shoulders: the entire indignation of the reader must be permitted
25 to concentrate on a single black nature.

13. Secret societies, camorras, mafias, et al., have no place in a detective story. Here the author gets into adventure fiction and secret-service romance. A fascinating and truly beautiful murder

---

1 **to disperse sth** to spread sth around; break sth up into pieces – 3 **to pit one's mind against sb/ sth** *sich mit jdm/ etw messen* – 6 **relay team** group of people who each run a part of a race *(Staffelmannschaft)* – 19 **sordid** disreputable, dirty – 19 **menial** servant – 20 **to embalm** to envelop, to wrap sth up (in order to preserve it for ever) – 23 **onus** responsibility – 26 **camorra** Italian crime syndicate

is irremediably spoiled by any such wholesale culpability. To be sure, the murderer in a detective novel should be given a sporting chance, but it is going too far to grant him a secret society (with its ubiquitous havens, mass protection, etc.) to fall back on. No
5 high-class, self-respecting murderer would want such odds in his jousting-bout with the police.

14. The method of murder, and the means of detecting it, must be rational and scientific. That is to say, pseudo-science and purely imaginative and speculative devices are not to be
10 tolerated in the roman policier. For instance, the murder of a victim by a newly found element – a super-radium, let us say – is not a legitimate problem. Nor may a rare and unknown drug, which has its existence only in the author's imagination, be
15 administered. A detective-story writer must limit himself, toxicologically speaking, to the pharmacopoeia. Once an author soars into the realm of fantasy, in the Jules Verne manner, he is outside the bounds of detective fiction, cavorting in the uncharted reaches of adventure.

15. The truth of the problem must at all times be apparent –
20 provided the reader is shrewd enough to see it. By this I mean that if the reader, after learning the explanation for the crime, should reread the book, he would see that the solution had, in a sense, been staring him in the face – that all the clues really pointed to the culprit – and that, if he had been as clever as the
25 detective, he could have solved the mystery himself without going on to the final chapter. That the clever reader does often

---

1 **irremediably** [ˌɪrɪˈmiːdiəbli] irreversibly *(nicht behebbar)* – 4 **ubiquitous** [juːˈbɪkwɪtəs] always present – 4 **haven** [ˈheɪvᵊn] place of refuge – 6 **jousting-bout** duel, fight – 10 **roman policier** *(Fr)* crime novel – 15 **toxicologically** [ˌtɒksɪkᵊlˈɒdʒɪkᵊli] with reference to poison – 15 **pharmacopoeia** a book describing drugs, chemicals and medicinal preparations – 16 **to soar** *(fig)* to fly, glide upwards – 16 **Jules Verne** (1828–1905) French novelist, poet and playwright best known for his surrealist adventure novels. Seen as one of the founders of modern science fiction. – 17 **to cavort in** to move around in a playful but chaotic way – 18 **uncharted** unexplored – 20 **shrewd** [ʃruːd] clever

thus solve the problem goes without saying. And one of my basic theories of detective fiction is that, if a detective story is fairly and legitimately constructed, it is impossible to keep the solution from all readers. There will inevitably be a certain number of 5 them just as shrewd as the author; and if the author has shown the proper sportsmanship and honesty in his statement and projection of the crime and its clues, these perspicacious readers will be able, by analysis, elimination and logic, to put their finger on the culprit as soon as the detective does. And herein lies the 10 zest of the game. Herein we have an explanation for the fact that readers who would spurn the ordinary "popular" novel will read detective stories unblushingly.

16. A detective novel should contain no long, descriptive passages, no literary dallying with side-issues, no subtly worked- 15 out character analyses, no "atmospheric" preoccupations. Such matters have no vital place in a record of crime and deduction. They hold up the action, and introduce issues irrelevant to the main purpose, which is to state a problem, analyze it, and bring it to a successful conclusion. To be sure, there must be a sufficient 20 descriptiveness and character delineation to give the novel verisimilitude; but when an author of a detective story has reached that literary point where he has created a gripping sense of reality and enlisted the reader's interest and sympathy in the characters and the problem, he has gone as far in the purely 25 "literary" technique as is legitimate and compatible with the needs of a criminal-problem document. A detective story is a grim business, and the reader goes to it, not for literary furbelows and beautiful descriptions, but for mental stimulation and intellectual activity – just as he goes to a ball game or to a cross- 30 word puzzle. Lectures between innings at the Polo Grounds on

---

7 **perspicacious** [ˌpɜːspɪˈkeɪʃəs] far-sighted – 10 **zest** appeal – 11 **to spurn** to reject –
12 **unblushingly** *here:* without hesitation, without shame – 14 **to dally** *(inf)* to waste
time – 20 **delineation** *here:* portrayal, description – 21 **verisimilitude** [ˌverɪsɪˈmɪlɪtjuːd]
authenticity – 27 **furbelows** *here:* embellishment, decoration

the beauties of nature would scarcely enhance the interest in
the struggle between two contesting baseball teams; and
dissertations on etymology and orthography in the definitions
of a cross-word puzzle would tend only to irritate the solver
5   bent on making the words interlock correctly.

17. A professional criminal must never be shouldered with the
guilt of a crime in a detective story. Crimes by house-breakers
and bandits are the province of the police department – not of
authors and brilliant amateur detectives. Such crimes belong to
10 the routine work of the Homicide Bureaus. A really fascinating
crime is one committed by a pillar of a church, or a spinster
noted for her charities.

18. A crime in a detective story must never turn out to be an
accident or a suicide. To end an odyssey of sleuthing with such
15 an anti-climax is to play an unpardonable trick on the reader.
If a book-buyer should demand his two dollars back on the
grounds that the crime was a fake, any court with a sense of
justice would decide in his favor and add a stinging reprimand
to the author who thus hoodwinked a trusting and kind-hearted
20 reader.

19. The motives for all crimes in detective stories should be
personal. International plottings and war politics belong in a
different category of fiction – in secret-service tales, for instance.
But a murder story must be kept gemütlich, so to speak. It must
25 reflect the reader's everyday experiences, and give him a certain
outlet for his own repressed desires and emotions.

20. And (to give my Credo an even score of items) I now list a
few devices which no self-respecting detective-story writer

---

10 **Homicide Bureau** *(AE)* police division responsible for the solving of murders – 11 **pillar of
a church** *here:* an important person in the Church hierarchy – 11 **spinster** unmarried
woman, old maid – 14 **sleuthing** detecting; crime solving – 18 **reprimand** rebuke *(Rüge)* –
19 **to hoodwink** to trick, to betray – 24 **gemütlich** *The author probably means here:*
"personal" or "close to home" – 27 **Credo** [ˈkreɪdəʊ] set of principles, beliefs or rules

will avail himself of. They have been used too often, and are familiar to all true lovers of literary crime. To use them is a confession of the author's ineptitude and lack of originality:

(a) Determining the identity of the culprit by comparing the
5 butt of a cigarette left at the scene of the crime with the brand smoked by a suspect.

(b) The bogus spiritualistic séance to frighten the culprit into giving himself away.

(c) Forged finger-prints.

10 (d) The dummy-figure alibi.

(e) The dog that does not bark and thereby reveals the fact that the intruder is familiar.

(f) The final pinning of the crime on a twin, or a relative who looks exactly like the suspected, but innocent, person.

15 (g) The hypodermic syringe and the knockout drops.

(h) The commission of the murder in a locked room after the police have actually broken in.

(i) The word-association test for guilt.

(j) The cipher, or code letter, which is eventually unraveled by
20 the sleuth.

(First published in "American Magazine" in 1928 and reprinted in "The Winter Murder Case".)

---

1 **to avail oneself of sth** *(fml)* to use sth – 3 **ineptitude** lack of ability – 7 **bogus** ['bəʊgəs] fake – 13 **to pin sth on sb** to blame sb for sth, to make sb responsible for sth – 15 **hypodermic syringe** [ˌhaɪpəˌdɜːmɪk.sɪˈrɪndʒ] medical device used to inject into or withdraw fluids from the body – 19 **to unravel** to solve

2. A Detective Story Decalogue (1929)

English clergyman and crime author Ronald Knox (1888–1957)
compiled this ten-rule list for Golden Age mysteries only one year
after Van Dine, mirroring the Ten Commandments.

5 1. The criminal must be mentioned near the beginning of the
story, but readers must not be able to read his or her
thoughts.
2. There must be no events that cannot be explained by natural
laws (e.g. the murderer walked through a solid wall to commit
10 the crime).
3. An absolute maximum of one secret room or passage is
allowed.
4. No hitherto unknown poisons may be used, nor any machine
or contraption which will need a long scientific explanation at
15 the end.
5. No Chinaman must have a significant role in the story.
6. No accident must ever help the detective, nor must he ever
have an unaccountable intuition which proves to be right.
7. The detective must not himself commit the crime.
20 8. The detective must not suddenly discover any clues which
are not immediately allowed to be inspected by the reader.
9. The stupid friend of the detective (the Watson) must not hide
any thoughts to do with the crime from the reader, and he must
be slightly, but very slightly, less intelligent than the average
25 reader.
10. Twin brothers, and doubles generally, must not figure in the
story unless we have been properly prepared for them.

(*Originally published in "Best Detective Stories of 1928–29"*)

---

1 **decalogue** *(Rel)* The Ten Commandments – 13 **hitherto** [ˌhɪðəˈtuː] until this point –
18 **unaccountable** inexplicable

3. Ten Commandments for the Detective Novel (1949)

1. It must have credible motivation, both in terms of the original situation and of the dénouement.

2. It must be technically sound in terms of methods of murder and detection.

3. It must be realistic in its characters, settings and atmosphere. It must be about real people in a real world.

4. It must have good story value, even without the mystery element. In other words, the investigation itself must be an adventure that is truly worth reading.

5. It must be simple enough to be explained easily when the time comes.

6. It must confuse and challenge a reasonably intelligent reader.

7. The solution must seem inevitable – even obvious – once it is revealed.

8. It must not try to do everything at once. If it is a puzzle which operates in a somewhat cool, reasonable atmosphere, it cannot also be a violent adventure or a passionate romance.

9. It must punish the criminal in some way, but not necessarily by use of the law of the land. If the detective fails to resolve the consequences of the crime, the story remains somehow unresolved, and this will irritate the reader.

10. It must be honest with the reader.

(Based on Raymond Chandler's "Twelve Notes on the Mystery Novel")

---

4 **dénouement** *(Fr)* [deɪˈnuːmãːŋ] conclusion of a drama (revelation, resolution or catastrophe) – 5 **sound** reasonable, credible